Chain and Bead Jewelry

Geometric Connections

WATSON-GUPTILL PUBLICATIONS / NEW YORK

Chain and Bead Jewelry

Geometric Connections

A NEW ANGLE ON CREATING DIMENSIONAL

EARRINGS, BRACELETS, AND NECKLACES

Scott David Plumlee

Text and step-by-step photography copyright © 2010 by Scott David Plumlee
Photography of finished jewelry copyright © 2010 by Watson-Guptill Publications

Published in 2010 by Watson-Guptill Publications,
an imprint of Crown Publishing, a division of Random House, Inc.
1745 Broadway, New York, NY 10019
www.crownpublishing.com
www.watsonguptill.com

WATSON-GUPTILL is a registered trademark and the WG
and Horse designs are trademarks of Random House, Inc., New York.

Library of Congress Cataloging-in-Publication Data

Plumlee, Scott David.
 Chain and bead jewelry geometric connections : a new angle on creating dimensional earrings,
bracelets, and necklaces / Scott David Plumlee.
 p. cm.
 Includes index.
 ISBN 978-0-8230-3339-3
 1. Jewelry making. 2. Metal-work. 3. Beadwork. I. Title.
 TT212.P543 2010
 739.27--dc22
 2009049289

Cover Design: veést design
Designer: Chin-Yee Lai
Photographers: Simon Lee; Scott David Plumlee
Printed in China

First printing, 2010

1 2 3 4 5 6 7 8 9 / 18 17 16 15 14 13 12 11 10

Acknowledgments

I wish to dedicate this book to everyone who believed in me, especially:

- My loving parents, Larry and Shirley, for their encouragement and support
- My brother Jeff; his wife, Erika; and their two boys, Isaac and Nathan, for all the smiles
- All the students who took workshops and encouraged me to write this book series
- All the patrons who purchased my jewelry art and invested in my business
- All the teaching institutions that invited me to lead jewelry-making workshops
- All the fine art galleries that retail my jewelry and provide representation
- Joy Aquilino and all the fine folks at Watson-Guptill / Crown / Random House
- Martha Moran for the extraordinary dedication to editing the manuscript
- Tim Sheriff at Swanstrom Tools, for all the hard work on the mandrel-tip pliers
- Anthony Squillacci at APAC, for making my findings and student supply kits
- Sophie Lenoir, for the rooftop photo shoot to capture my face in front of Taos Mountain
- Spider, for gifting me the jump rings to make almost all of the projects in this book

Contents

Preface

Welcome to a new plateau of creativity, where shiny metal jump rings and yummy gemstone beads are combined in endless possibilities. Come explore this new horizon with me, as I lead you down a chain-making trail in a jewelry-designing adventure. This is my third book in a series that is dedicated to beaded chain jewelry design, expanding my published repertoire into a sophisticated series of geometry-inspired shapes and patterns.

The art of geometry has always been inspired by nature's own delicate designs yet perfected by man's compass and ruler upon paper. Geometry has been utilized throughout history to create our most eye-catching architecture—from the Egyptian pyramids and European quatrefoil fountains to Washington, DC's Pentagon. These geometric shapes have captured our imagination, and now you can use geometry to your benefit to create stunning jewelry for yourself and your loved ones.

The first two chapters cover metal wire and bead basics, the simple hand tools required, and then continue into the essential chain-making and bead-setting techniques. These skills are put into practice in the third chapter, as the age-old Byzantine chain leads into singular, paired, serrated, and tripled chain patterns. Following this introduction section, the three-way Tripoli formation is illustrated step-by-step to serve as the backbone chain component of the geometric patterns to follow.

This three-way Tripoli formation is utilized individually, paired, and offset with a variety of bead-embellishment techniques as we build momentum into more dimensional jewelry designs. Next, we assemble three Tripoli forms into a Triangle form with a center spiral and explore how this Triangle form can be used individually, as a necklace centerpiece, or doubled-up and repeated into a wide bracelet pattern that connects with a side-by-side magnetic clasping system.

Following this formula, we transcend into using four Tripoli forms to build a four-sided Quatrefoil form and the Trapezoid Bracelet, then five Tripoli forms to build a Pentagon form. The beaded geometric shapes will continue to evolve into the centerpiece of the Pentagram Necklace. Finally, the last chapter, Organic Formations, illustrates a four-way formation into the Fish pattern, a five-way and six-way formation into the Snowflake pattern, and culminating with the Butterfly Necklace centerpiece that has two levels of bead embellishment.

The appendix outlines the basics of making your own headpins from Argentium sterling silver wire. There are illustrated chain configurations at the end of the book, which I think you'll refer to often, as well as a resource section that tells you where you can find all the tools and materials used for the projects in this book. **Note:** For those of you working in the metric system, please refer to the metric conversion chart on page 19.

Thank you. I hope you get as much satisfaction using this book as I did creating it.

Sincerely jazzed,

Scott David Plumlee

1 Chain and Bead Basics

The fundamental elements of beaded chain jewelry are metal wire jump rings and gemstone beads. Before we work on techniques and create jewelry pieces, let's take some time to explore the multitude of aesthetic options offered by different metal wires (red copper, brown bronze, 14/20 gold filled, and Argentium sterling silver) in combination with a variety of gemstone beads. We also discuss all the hand tools and finishing processes you'll need, from mandrels, pliers, and calipers to pickling pots and rotary tumblers.

METAL WIRE

Metal wire is the essential component in chain making, and the metals you use must strike a delicate balance between being soft enough to allow jump rings to open and close without breaking and being strong enough to hold the ring's round shape and create a sturdy unsoldered chain. Pure metals are for the most part too soft for chain making, so we work with metal alloys, which are composed of several metals that have been melted together to produce a superior end product. Here are some of the metal alloys produced in wire form that I like to work with—bronze, copper, gold, and silver.

Bronze Wire

Jewelry bronze, actually a brass alloy, also known as NuGold, low brass, and Merlin's Gold, is composed of smelting 85 percent copper with 15 percent zinc. Jewelry bronze is slightly darker than standard yellow brass, which tarnishes quite readily to a rich, warm brown color.

Copper Wire

Copper is a pure metal, which becomes a brass when alloyed. In its pure form, it is quite inexpensive and readily available. Although softer than sterling silver, it is invaluable for testing designs and for beginners to practice with. Copper is a highly reactive metal that will darken with exposure to the elements and will turn the wearer's skin green as it oxidizes.

14/20 Gold-Filled Wire

Gold-filled (GF) wire has a layer of gold alloy bonded to the outside of a base wire. With 14/20 GF wire, $1/20^{th}$ of the wire's weight ratio is a thin layer of 14-karat gold that is heat and pressure bonded to the outside of a cheaper metal base wire, typically brass. Since the base metal is sealed within the bonded gold, it cannot leach out and tarnish the wire. If you want the look of gold without the huge cost, this option is ideal.

Note: Gold-*plating* is a thin layer of gold that has been electronically plated over a base metal. It is not advisable for jump rings, as the rings will rub together and quickly remove the gold layer.

Argentium Sterling Silver

Argentium sterling silver is a patented and trademarked alloy that is 92.5 percent pure silver, just like traditional sterling silver. What makes it different is that a small amount of germanium metalloid replaces some of the copper that is usually the other 7.5 percent of sterling silver. Here are just a few of the amazing working properties and specialized techniques that Argentium offers.

Tarnish Resistance: The most important reason to use Argentium over traditional sterling is the tarnish resistance that results from proper heat treatment (see page 18); its ability to hold a polished shine (see page 153) and resist oxidation darkening is unparalleled.

Teardropping Head Pins: The second great feature of Argentium wire is that it makes perfectly smooth teardrop-shaped balls at the ends of wires, allowing you to create your own headpins from any gauge of wire (see page 154).

Ductility and Malleability: Argentium has a greater ductility (the ability to be stretched or elongated) and malleability (the ability to be transformed when forged with a hammer and anvil, such as for an S-clasp—see page 29).

GEMSTONE BEADS

Semiprecious gemstone beads are visually attractive and physically long lasting and have been attributed with a wide range of metaphysical properties. Although once a status symbol of kings and queens, you can now find a mind-numbing assortment of gemstone beads at your local bead shop, craft stores, online, and through catalog companies (see references on page 155).

Beads by definition have a hole drilled through them so they can be strung together. While there is no industrywide standard for the size of the hole, it typically ranges from 0.75mm to 1mm in diameter. If a bead's hole does not allow a headpin wire to pass through, use a smaller gauge headpin or enlarge the hole with a diamond-plated bead-reaming bit in an electric screwdriver.

A gemstone's hardness is rated on the Mohs rating system from 1 to 10, with 1 being soft talc and 10 being diamond hardness. I typically use gemstones with a 7 Mohs hardness, such as carnelian, amethyst, onyx, quartz, and agate, which are unaffected by being polished with steel-shot in a rotary tumbler. Softer gemstones with 5 to 6 Mohs hardness, such as turquoise, lapis lazuli, and hematite, will loose their shine in the steel-shot but can be polished with rice in a rotary tumbler (see page 18).

Black Hematite is an opaque gemstone that is typically gun-metal gray-black with a metallic luster. The Beaded (9) Tripoli Earrings design utilizes hematite beads alongside blue turquoise beads. Hematite and turquoise complement each other quite well but are both relatively soft, so don't tumble them with steel-shot; use rice.

Black Onyx is an opaque gemstone that is naturally banded with grays but is typically dyed to a solid black with a glossy, glasslike shine. I used faceted black onyx beads in bronze Fish formations in the Fish Bracelet, the Pentagram Necklace, the gold Six-Pointed Snowflake formations, and the Butterfly Necklace centerpiece.

Blue Chalcedony is a translucent gemstone that can range from a gray-blue to a medium blue. The Butterfly Necklace centerpiece uses a pair of round chalcedony beads; the Japanese Rose Necklace uses a large cabochon, hanging below the center Triangle formation.

Blue Lapis Lazuli is less of a gemstone and more of a rock that ranges from a royal blue to baby blue in color, typically with metallic pyrite inclusions and a greasy luster. The Incan Triangle Necklace and the Quatrefoil Earrings use round blue lapis lazuli beads that look very regal set inside the silver-and-gold chain design. It is a softer stone, so don't tumble it with steel-shot; use rice.

Blue Quartz is a translucent quartz gemstone that ranges from natural sky blues to a variety of chemically enhanced regal blues. The Triple Byzantine Key Fob is set with faceted blue quartz beads, the Suspended Tripoli Bracelet with blue quartz barrels, and the Byzantine Cross Earrings with round blue quartz beads, as are several silver Fish formations in the Fish Bracelet.

Blue Turquoise is an opaque gemstone that can range from blue-green to a sky blue, with flecks of pyrite or veins of dark limonite and a waxy luster. I used blue turquoise beads in the Trapezoid Key Fob and the Beaded (9) Tripoli Earrings. It is a softer stone, so don't tumble it with steel-shot; use rice.

Green Aventurine is an opaque gemstone that ranges from a verdant to an olive green. I used a variety of aventurine beads in the Ocean Bracelet.

Green Chrysoprase is an opaque gemstone that can range from apple green to a darker green. The Double Pentagon Bracelet, the copper Five-Pointed Snowflake formation, and the Snowflake Bracelet are all embellished with round chrysoprase beads.

Green Jade is an opaque gemstone that can be red, black, or white but is typically green with a waxy shine. The Beaded Tripoli Earrings and Bracelet use green jade beads.

Purple Amethyst is a translucent gemstone that can range from high-grade deep royal lavender to a low-grade pale lilac. I use several sizes and shapes of amethyst beads throughout this book for different design applications—the Jens Pind Beaded Tripoli Bracelet, the Five-Pointed Snowflake formation, the Namaste Tripoli Bracelet, the Crystal Triangle Earrings, the Golden Triangle Necklace, and for the Butterfly Necklace centerpiece.

Red Carnelian is a translucent gemstone that can range from natural reddish-orange to a heat-treated cherry red. I used carnelian beads to embellish the Jens Pind Beaded Tripoli Bracelet, in the Double Pentagon Bracelet, the Snowflake Bracelet, the silver Five-Pointed Snowflakes, the Beaded Romanov Earrings, and the Butterfly centerpiece.

Red Garnet is a translucent gemstone that is a deep red, frequently with brown tint. The Pentagon Necklace and the Trapezoid Bracelet are set with round red garnet beads to complement the gold and silver chains.

Venetian Glass is technically not a gemstone but man-made beads from molten silica glass. The Ocean Bracelet uses a clear glass bead with blue swirl at the top of each Wave formation.

Gold or **Silver Magnetic** is not a gemstone but a cast bead of iron boron that has been magnetized and plated with gold or silver. They are used in magnetic clasps (see page 38). The Double Triangle Bracelet and the Pentagon Necklace both use a gold-plated magnetic clasp, the Butterfly Necklace uses a silver-plated magnetic clasp, and the Wide Triangle Bracelet uses two sets of silver-plated tube beads arranged in a unique magnetic clasping system.

TOOLS

Your tools are extensions of your fingers that are specialized to perform tasks that your hands alone just can't do. From the common paperclip to hammers and anvils to rotary drills and tumblers, here are all the tools you'll need to make chain and bead jewelry.

Mandrels

A jump ring's inside diameter will be almost the same diameter as the mandrel used to create it. Wire-wrapping mandrels are available in both millimeter and fractions-of-an-inch sizes. The ruler (below) provides both millimeter and inch measurements to show how they compare. The left side lists diameters in ¼-millimeter (0.25mm) increments; the right side lists diameters in ¹⁄₆₄-inch (0.40mm) increments. The far right column lists the millimeter equivalent for each fraction-of-an-inch size.

Millimeters	Inches	(metric size)
2mm	5/64"	(1.98mm)
2.25mm		
2.5mm	3/32"	(2.38mm)
2.75mm	7/64"	(2.78mm)
3mm		
3.25mm	1/8"	(3.18mm)
3.5mm	9/64"	(3.57mm)
3.75mm		
4mm	5/32"	(3.96mm)
4.25mm		
4.5mm	11/64"	(4.37mm)
4.75mm	3/16"	(4.76mm)
5mm		
5.25mm	13/64"	(5.16mm)
5.5mm	7/32"	(5.56mm)
5.75mm		
6mm	15/64"	(5.95mm)
6.25mm	1/4"	(6.35mm)
6.5mm		
6.75mm	17/64"	(6.75mm)
7mm		
	9/32"	(7.14mm)
7.5mm	19/64"	(7.54mm)
8mm	5/16"	(7.94mm)

Mandrel Size Chart

Bending mandrels are used to bend wires. Convenient mandrels for bending earring backs are a 2.35mm (³⁄₃₂-inch) steel rod and 8mm round plastic mechanical pencils.

Knitting needle mandrels are great for wrapping. A wrapping mandrel is a round metal rod around which wire is wrapped in a continuous coil before it is cut into individual jump rings. Aluminum knitting needles work well for wrapping, but don't use bamboo or plastic needles. Knitting needles come in a variety of sizes at your local knitting and fabric stores. For easy identification, I label each mandrel with its mm size.

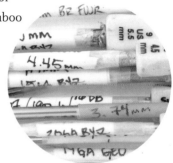

Knitting needle mandrels

Note: Never trust the stated millimeter size on a package of knitting needles; instead, measure the needles with digital calipers and label them with their actual millimeter size.

Power mandrels wrap wire much faster than you can by hand. A great tool for wrapping wire to be cut into jump rings (see page 23) is a 3.6-volt electric screwdriver with a hex-base, three-prong chuck adaptor. This type of chuck holds a variety of mandrel sizes, and the space between the three prongs holds the end of the wire, maintaining the spring tension as the coil is wrapped.

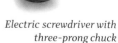

Electric screwdriver with three-prong chuck

Flat-nose pliers   *Chain-nose pliers*   *Round-nose pliers*   *Side cutters*

Hand Tools

I find that quality hand tools decrease frustration and increase the quality of my students' jewelry. I prefer American-made Swanstrom pliers because they are comfortable to use and will last a lifetime. Tool companies are listed in the resources section on page 155.

Flat-nose pliers are used in every project. Two flat-nose pliers work in tandem to open and close jump rings with a broad grip on both sides of the jump ring.

Pointed chain-nose pliers are more appropriate for working with finer gauge wire, smashing crimp tubes, and getting into a tight chain pattern to close that last pesky jump ring.

Round-nose pliers have tapered jaws, which yield many diameters. If you want a consistent diameter in a wire loop, you must keep the wire at a specific place on the jaw. Make a temporary diameter mark with a felt-tip marker or a permanent one with the edge of a file.

Mandrel-tip pliers are for setting beads. I assisted Swanstrom Tool Company in developing them. One mandrel jaw is a consistent 3.1mm, and the other jaw is a consistent 3.9mm diameter, which allows you to wrap perfect double-loop bead settings (see page 36). Mandrel-tip pliers, with 3.5mm and 4.5mm jaws are also available.

Side cutters, aka flush cutters, are available in several sizes, each for a specific range of wire sizes.

Other Tools

These tools, designed to simplify the jewelry-making process, should be thought of as extensions of your hands and eyes. Being a minimalist with tools and techniques allows the finished work to have a handcrafted look and feel.

Beading cable

Beading cable is a multistrand, nylon-coated stainless steel braided cable that is used to set beads into the chain design, secured with a smashed crimp tube. There is a wide variety of strand counts, diameters, and finish colors of beading cable available. I use the 19-strand, 0.012-inch (0.30mm) diameter, with a clear nylon finish. Use the chain-nose pliers, rather than your fingers, when pushing the beading cable through the chain patterns, into gemstone beads, and through tiny crimp tubes.

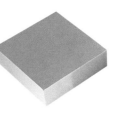

Bench block anvil

The bench block anvil sits on top of your work surface. It is made of polished steel and is generally about 4 × 4 inches and ¾-inch thick. You use this with the planishing hammer to forge an S-clasp (see page 29).

Mandrel-tip pliers   *Crimp tubes*

Planishing hammer

Optivisors   *Digital calipers*

Crimp tubes are tiny millimeter-length tubes that are used in tandem with the beading cable to secure gemstone beads to a chain. Crimp tubes are available in a wide variety of metals and sizes. The ones shown (page 16) are sterling silver tubes that are 1mm in diameter with an inside diameter hole of 0.030 inch (0.76mm). Notice that the inside diameter is two times larger than the beading cable's diameter, which allows just enough room for the cable to pass through the crimp tube twice and hold securely when smashed.

Digital calipers are ideal for precise measurement of wire and mandrel diameters and the inside diameter of jump rings.

Felt-tip markers are used to mark diameters on the round-nose pliers' jaws and for marking specific lengths on a wire for precise wire bending to set gemstones.

Flat jewelry files are used to remove any burrs from the ring joint.

Folding lamps offer good lighting, which is critical for seeing the subtle details of jump ring assembly.

Folding lamp

Flat jewelry files

Frisbee discs are perfect for holding your beads, headpins, jump rings, and extra pliers during assembly, and when the phone rings all the materials and tools for the project are in one location.

Fabric measuring tape, due to its flexibility, is perfect for measuring curved wire and can be cut to the length you need.

Optivisors are magnifiers worn to help you focus on the fine detail of where a ring is being positioned within a chain pattern and to get a proper closure on each individual jump ring.

Paperclips may surprise you, but I give out lots of them when I teach workshops, and I recommend that beginners start their chain designs with a paperclip to identify a beginning point.

A planishing hammer is used, in conjunction with a bench block anvil, to flatten head pins and wires, form S-clasps, and to remove irregular indentations and bumps in metal.

Sanding pads, 320-grit "superfine," are used to smooth each jump ring's joint; this scuffing will polish out in the steel-shot tumbling, creating visually seamless rings. They are sold as 4 × 5-inch pads but can be easily cut into smaller 1 × 2-inch swatches.

Storage containers can be used to store beads and rings, particularly see-through stacking plastic bins and in sealable plastic bags. Metal rings are rough on plastic bags, so use 4mm thickness or freezer bags to prevent holes (and losing all your marbles).

FINISHING PROCESSES

A home oven is all you need to perform this precipitation-hardening process for Argentium sterling silver. Place the finished jewelry in a clean, glass baking dish. Set the oven to 450°F (230°C) and bake for two hours. When the metal cools, the surface may have a slight yellow tint. Remove it with a warm pickle solution and then polish the metal to a high shine in a rotary tumbler.

Note: Magnetic beads lose their polarity during heating, and soft minerals, like turquoise and lapis lazuli, can burn in the heating process and lose their shine in the tumbler.

A pickle pot is an acid-water solution that deoxidizes metal. You can use a small slow cooker with a ceramic liner, but it is imperative that it is dedicated for nonfood use ONLY and that you label the pot with a poison symbol. The dry grains of acid are available from a jewelry supply store; always add acid to water, following manufacturer's instructions. Using the timer, set the dedicated slow cooker for one hour to warm (yet never boil) the solution; it will stay warm all day without drying out. Using tongs, dip the jewelry in and out of the solution for about thirty seconds. When finished, neutralize all jewelry and utensils with baking soda and rinse thoroughly under tap water.

Rotary tumblers, designed for polishing rocks into gems, can also be used with stainless steel-shot to produce a high shine on your finished jewelry designs. Fill the rubber barrel halfway with shot and two-thirds with water. Add your chain and a dab of liquid hand soap and let it spin for thirty minutes for a "bling-bling" shine. The longer you run the tumbler, the stronger the metal will get (even for days).

Lortone manufactures quality rotary tumblers in a variety of sizes and load capacities. This longer model can hold two or three barrels, so you can use one barrel for rice, another barrel for steel-shot, and a third dedicated to patina process. If you need to tumble more than two or three bracelets at a time, you may want to opt for Lortone's larger A4 model, which can handle three times as many silver bracelets and has a ten-sided interior that increases the tumbling action.

SOME TUMBLING TRICKS OF THE TRADE

- Use a metal coffee filter to strain the water from the shot and chain. You can reuse the tumbling water until it turns black.
- Make sure you purchase *stainless* steel-shot or it will rust over time.
- Get a variety of steel-shot shapes, including balls and pins, for a superior polish.
- Sun or oven dry (150°F / 65°C) your steel-shot and store it in an airtight container when not tumbling.
- When polishing loose, unassembled jump rings, don't add steel-shot or you will spend hours separating the two. Just tumble the jump rings alone in water. To speed up the process, tumble them with a three-ring interwoven Flower (see page 28).
- Use dry rice, without water, to tumble chains that have soft bead embellishments; steel-shot will harm softer minerals like lapis lazuli, turquoise, and hematite.

Inches to Centimeters		Centimeters to Inches	
Inches	CM	CM	Inches
1/8	0.32	1	3/8
1/4	0.64	2	3/4
3/8	0.95	3	1 1/8
7/16	1.11	4	1 5/8
1/2	1.27	5	2
5/8	1.59	6	2 3/8
3/4	1.91	7	2 1/4
7/8	2.22	8	3 1/8
1	2.54	9	3 1/2
2	5.08	10	4
3	7.65	11	4 3/8
4	10.16	12	4 3/4
5	12.70	13	5 1/8
6	15.24	14	5 1/2
7	17.78	15	5 7/8
8	20.32	16	6 1/4
9	22.66	17	6 3/4
10	25.40	18	7 1/8
11	27.94	19	7 1/2
12	30.48	20	7 7/8

JEWELER'S JOURNAL

I keep an 8 x 10 sketchpad or blank book as a journal to document my jewelry design explorations. When inspiration hits, I loosely sketch necklace designs or chain patterns that have been forming in my mind's eye and then brainstorm, without prejudgment, on various ways to create them. I spend extensive trial-and-error hours in the studio testing various solutions and keep detailed notes of all wire and ring measurements used in each experiment. If a design I create is successful, I can reproduce the entire process with the same results; if the design still needs work, I can use the data to make educated decisions for the next experiment.

2 Essential Techniques

The essential component of chain making is the sizing of the individual jump rings that will be assembled link by link into a prescribed chain pattern. In this chapter, I explain aspect ratio in simple language, discuss how metal wire thickness is sized, give a tutorial on wrapping wire and cutting jump rings, and list the appropriate inside diameter and wire thickness of the jump rings used in each of the chain patterns featured in this book. I take you on through illustrated course in proper jump ring and headpin utilization, from the basics to spiraling rings together into Flower forms and setting gemstone beads and magnetic clasps with single-, double-, and triple-loop-around techniques. In the Beaded Single-Chain Bracelet, we assemble single loop-around bead settings into a Single chain. We make a companion pair of Beaded Single-Chain Earrings, with detailed instructions on how to make matching earring backs. Once you have mastered these basic skills, you will be ready to tackle all the jewelry designs in this book with confidence.

JUMP RING THEORY

Chain jewelry is based on assembling individual metal jump rings, link by link, to create a linear length of flexible metal in a consistent pattern. The greatest frustration to the novice chain maker and expert jeweler alike is determining the correct size of the jump ring that will allow the successful assembly of a particular chain pattern. Each chain design has an established aspect ratio (AR) sizing (see page 24); if you use jump rings that deviate too far from the recommended AR sizing, the chain will be difficult to assemble, appear out of proportion (too tight or too loose), or both. The brass jump ring (below) illustrates the two key components of AR: the diameter of the wire's thickness and the jump ring's inside diameter (ID). Dividing the jump ring's ID by the wire's diameter will give you the numerical value of the ring's AR. For example, a jump ring with a 4.5mm ID made from 16-gauge (1.3mm diameter) wire has an AR of 3.4 (4.5 ÷ 1.3 = 3.44). This information is critical, regardless of whether you choose to purchase jump rings or make your own. (For an overview of wrapping and cutting jump rings, see page 23.)

Premade Jump Rings

If you choose to buy premade rings, be aware that each manufacturer has its own system for measuring them. Some measure the jump ring's inside diameter, whereas others measure its outer diameter. Some measure their jump rings in inches, some in millimeters; a few do both.

You should also note that jump rings are sometimes actually larger than the stated size of wrapping mandrel due to the "spring back" of the coiled metal wire. This spring-back effect occurs whenever wire is coil wrapped, but it can be intensified when work-hardened wire is used or when rings of large diameter are wrapped. For instance, 19-gauge wire wrapped on an 8mm mandrel will produce a jump ring that has an 8.5-9mm inside diameter.

jump ring's inside diameter

wire diameter

Kerfless jump ring

Saw-cut jump ring

Jump rings can also be slightly smaller than the stated circumference of the wrapped mandrel when the coil is saw cut, which creates a "kerf," or gap, in the circumference of the ring where it's cut from the coil. When the kerf is closed, it results in a slightly smaller—and slightly oval—ring. The thickness of the jump ring's kerf depends on the thickness of the saw blade, the technique used to cut it, and level of the manufacturer's quality control.

To overcome these inconsistencies when using purchased jump rings, I look for those that are "perfectly round" and "kerfless" and whose measurements are precise to 1/100 of a millimeter, so that their closed ID is exactly as stated on the packaging. For a list of manufacturers, see the resources on page 155.

Jump rings, from left to right: brass, gold, silver, and copper

Jump Ring Gauge

Round wire is measured in thickness increments (gauges) by the American Wire Gauge (AWG) number system, which is also known as the Brown and Sharpe system. The European Union (EU) metric system measures wire thickness increments by millimeter (mm) diameters that are relatively close to AWG wires. At right is a table that lists the AWG numerical gauge sizes and the corresponding diameters in millimeters and the EU metric system counterpart.

Wire can be purchased at different levels of hardness. "Dead-soft" wire has been heat treated in an annealing process to reduce the stress within the metal. "Half-hard" wire has been pulled down four gauge sizes, and "hard" wire has been pulled down roughly eight gauge sizes. I recommend using half-hard silver, bronze, or gold for the correct balance between being too soft so that the rings deform or too hard so that the rings get brittle.

AWG	dot	MM	EU
10	●	2.54	2.5
11	●	2.25	n/a
12	●	2.00	2.0
13	●	1.83	1.8
14	●	1.63	1.6
15	●	1.45	1.5
16	●	1.25	1.3
17	•	1.15	1.1
18	•	1.00	1.0
19	•	0.91	0.9
20	•	0.81	0.8
21	•	0.72	0.7
22	•	0.63	0.6
23	.	0.57	n/a
24	.	0.50	0.5

WRAPPING AND CUTTING JUMP RINGS

If you have the "do it yourself" spirit and want to make your own jump rings, knock yourself out. I have been wrapping and cutting my own rings over the past decade, but after working 290 troy ounces of silver wire in 2007, I hired a manufacturer to make my jump rings. The question you have to ask yourself is, "What is my time worth?" If you really don't have the time to make your own, just order premade jump rings and save yourself the inherent frustrations of the AR blues. But if you want to make your own—here's an overview.

Jump rings can be cut from a coil with simple **side cutters**. The nipping action of the cutters leaves one side of the wire with a pointed burr and the opposite wire with a flat edge. If you want flush-cut rings, you must make two cuts per ring, cutting off a double-sided burr between each flush ring. Cutting jump rings by hand is time-consuming and requires hand-eye coordination to control the position of the cutter's blades to the coil.

Although **hand wrapping** wire into a coil is a slow and laborious chore, it doesn't require any electricity, and it will strengthen your handshake. Wrapping wire requires hand-eye coordination to guide the wire into a continuous coil without introducing any gaps or overlapping the wire.

A **3.6-volt electric screwdriver and three-prong chuck** are used to speed up the wire-wrapping process; this technique also achieves a tighter and more consistent coil. Grip the wire with a cloth to dissipate the friction, and take care when you reach the end of the wire, as it can cut your finger.

A **jeweler's frame saw** and fine-toothed blades can increase your cutting speed and yield more consistent flush-cut rings. Place the wrapped coil of wire onto the blade and then tighten the blade into the frame with the cutting teeth pointed inward. Place pressure with your thumb and first finger on the end six loops of the coil and saw them back and forth against the blade until they are cut off. Blade size #1 is appropriate for 20-, 19-, and 18-gauge wire; size #5 is suitable for 16-gauge; and size #6 for 14-gauge. Lubricating the blade with a wax product such as Bur-Life helps keep the saw blade cutting smoothly.

CALCULATING ASPECT RATIO

Below are a variety of chain patterns and their suggested aspect ratio (AR) sizing. I have listed all American Wire Gauge sizes from 20- to 14-gauge with their corresponding mandrel sizes to achieve the stated AR. The asterisks (*) indicate the jump ring sizes that are used in this book. For chain configurations, see pages 156-157.

You can make several different weaves with a single mandrel, provided that you use wire of different gauges. Inversely, if you have one gauge of wire, you can make several weaves as long as you have different mandrel sizes.

Single Chain

Aspect Ratio = 2.1 to 2.2

The Single chain has a simple 1+1+1 assembly.

20-gauge (0.8) on 1.75mm mandrel, AR = 2.2
19-gauge (0.9) on 2mm or $^5/_{64}$-inch mandrel, AR = 2.2
18-gauge (1.0) on 2.25mm mandrel, AR = 2.2
17-gauge (1.14) on 2.4mm mandrel or $^3/_{32}$-inch mandrel, AR = 2.1
*16-gauge (1.3) on 2.75mm or $^7/_{64}$-inch mandrel, AR = 2.1 or 2.13
15-gauge (1.45) on 3.1mm or $^1/_8$-inch mandrel, AR = 2.14 or 2.2
14-gauge (1.6) on 3.5mm or $^9/_{64}$-inch mandrel, AR = 2.15 or 2.2

Double Chain

Aspect Ratio = 3.0 to 3.1

The Double chain has a simple 2+2+2 assembly.

20-gauge (0.81) on 2.4mm or $^3/_{32}$-inch mandrel, AR = 3.0
19-gauge (0.91) on 2.75mm or $^7/_{64}$-inch mandrel, AR = 3.0
18-gauge (1.02) on 3.1mm or $^1/_8$-inch mandrel, AR = 3.0 or 3.1
17-gauge (1.14) on 3.5mm or $^9/_{64}$-inch mandrel, AR = 3.07 or 3.1
*16-gauge (1.3) on 4mm or $^5/_{32}$-inch mandrel, AR = 3.0 or 3.05
15-gauge (1.45) on 4.5mm or $^{11}/_{64}$-inch mandrel, AR = 3.1 or 3.0
14-gauge (1.63) on 5mm or $^{13}/_{64}$-inch mandrel, AR = 3.0 or 3.16

Jens Pind Chain

Aspect Ratio = 3.0 to 3.1

The Jens Pind chain uses the same size jump rings as the Double chain listed above.

Byzantine Chain

Aspect Ratio = 3.4 to 3.5

The Byzantine chain is aka the Birdcage, Idiot's Delight, and King's Braid.

*20-gauge (0.81) on a 2.75mm or $^7/_{64}$-inch mandrel, AR = 3.4
*19-gauge (0.91) on a 3.1mm or $^1/_8$-inch mandrel, AR = 3.4 or 3.5
*18-gauge (1.02) on a 3.5mm or $^9/_{64}$-inch mandrel, AR = 3.4 or 3.5
*17-gauge (1.14) on a 3.9mm or $^5/_{32}$-inch mandrel, AR = 3.4 or 3.5
*16-gauge (1.3) on a 4.5mm or $^{11}/_{64}$-inch mandrel, AR = 3.5 or 3.4
*15-gauge (1.45) on a 5mm or $^{13}/_{64}$-inch mandrel, AR = 3.5
*14-gauge (1.63) on a 5.5mm or $^7/_{32}$-inch mandrel, AR = 3.4

1+2+1 Chain

The 1+2+1 chain is assembled from two sizes of rings, one large ring connected by two smaller rings between. Use AR=3.5 Byzantine size rings in prescribed pairing as listed below.

    16-gauge, 4.5mm (single) with 20-gauge, 2.75mm (pair)
   *15-gauge, 5mm (single) with 19-gauge, 3.1mm (pair)
    14-gauge, 5.5mm (single) with 18-gauge, 3.5mm (pair)

Japanese 12-1 Chain

The Japanese 12-1 chain pattern is assembled into the Japanese Rose formation. Use AR=3.5 Byzantine size rings in prescribed pairings as listed above for the 1+2+1 chain.

Inca Puño Chain

Aspect Ratio = 4.3 to 4.4

The Inca Puño chain, aka Box chain or Queen's Link, is a repetitive pattern of four rings, assembled 2+2, and folded into knot forms.

    20-gauge (0.81) on 3.5mm or $^9/_{64}$-inch mandrel, AR = 4.3 or 4.4
    19-gauge (0.91) on 3.9mm or $^5/_{32}$-inch mandrel, AR = 4.3 or 4.35
   *18-gauge (1.02) on 4.5mm or $^{11}/_{64}$-inch mandrel, AR = 4.4 or 4.3
    17-gauge (1.14) on 5mm or $^{13}/_{64}$-inch mandrel, AR = 4.4 or 4.5
    16-gauge (1.3) on 5.5mm or $^7/_{32}$-inch mandrel, AR = 4.23 or 4.3
    15-gauge (1.45) on 6.3mm or $^1/_4$-inch mandrel, AR = 4.34 or 4.4
    14-gauge (1.63) on 7mm or $^9/_{32}$-inch mandrel, AR = 4.3 or 4.4

Three-Ring Flower Formation

Aspect Ratio = 4.3 to 4.4

A Flower formation is a spiraling of three rings, each added at the same spiraling angle so they lay into each other. Use AR=4.3 size rings, as listed above for the Inca Puño chain. For more on the Flower formation, see page 28.

Large Flower Formation

Aspect Ratio = 7.7 to 7.8

    20-gauge (0.81) on 6.3mm or $^1/_4$-inch mandrel, AR = 7.7 or 7.8
    19-gauge (0.91) on 7mm or $^9/_{32}$-inch mandrel, AR = 7.7 or 7.8
    18-gauge (1.02) on 8mm or $^5/_{16}$-inch mandrel, AR = 7.8
   *17-gauge (1.14) on 8.75mm or $^{11}/_{32}$-inch mandrel, AR = 7.7
    16-gauge (1.3) on 10mm or $^{25}/_{64}$-inch mandrel, AR = 7.7
    15-gauge (1.45) on 11mm or $^7/_{16}$-inch mandrel, AR = 7.6 or 7.7
    14-gauge (1.63) on 12.5mm or $^1/_2$-inch mandrel, AR = 7.7 or 7.8

Note: Due to the "spring back" created by the large diameter of the wrapping mandrels, the actual inside diameter of the Large Flower rings will be roughly $^1/_4$ to $^1/_2$ mm larger than the stated mandrel size.

WORKING WITH JUMP RINGS

A jump ring is a full circle of metal wire with a cut in the circumference that allows the ring to be twisted open, hooked into a chain, and then closed flush. They are the essential building blocks of any chain pattern, and understanding how to properly use and manipulate them will be the difference between your finished jewelry lasting a lifetime or unraveling. Here's an exercise that will help you perfect your technique.

Tools: Two flat-nose pliers.

Materials: Jump rings (any metal); larger gauges (14- and 15-gauge are easier for practicing than smaller gauges (18- and 19-gauge).

Note: Work with two flat-nose pliers, one in each hand. Instructions are given for left-handers in Step 3.

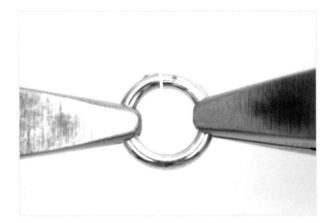

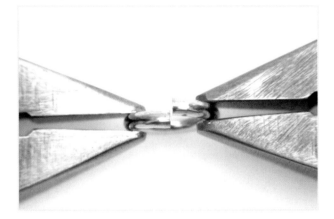

1 When you hold a jump ring in your flat-nose pliers, position the pliers' tips at three-o'clock and nine-o'clock, keeping the opening of the jump ring up at twelve-o'clock. This provides the best leverage on the ring and keeps your elbows up, allowing you to use your whole upper body to open and close the ring, versus using just your wrists.

2 Looking down on the jump ring, notice that the right side is naturally higher than the left; this is due to the direction the wire was wrapped before cutting. This is a standard in the jump ring–making industry. If you make your own jump rings and inadvertently wrap the rings in an opposite spiral, don't worry—either direction works.

3 Twist the jump ring open 30 degrees, *pulling* with the left pliers and *pushing* with the right pliers, both hands working simultaneously. **If you are left-handed**, reverse this by *pushing* with the left pliers and *pulling* with the right pliers, both hands working simultaneously.

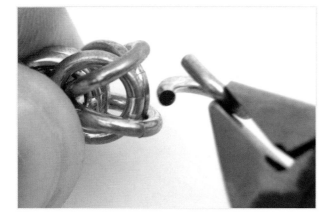

4 Always twist open jump rings with your dominate hand pushing away and nondominant hand pulling toward you. This lets you hold the open jump ring in your dominate hand's pliers, so you can feed the nondominant side of the jump ring (painted red) through the chain design. Notice the red dot on the cut edge (left side) of the open jump ring; this is the end of the open ring that must hook through the chain opening.

5 As each new jump ring is linked onto the chain, focus on the end of wire (red dot) to help you find the angle needed to hook through the chain opening.

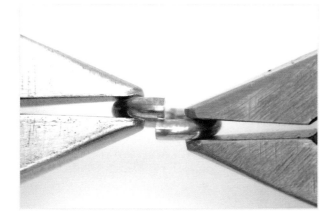

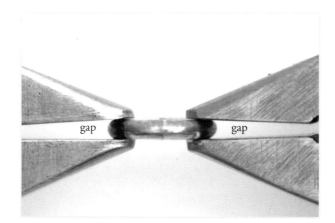

6 When closing jump rings, remember that wire has memory. Use flat-nose pliers to grip both sides of the open jump ring, and bring the right tip below and just past the left tip to counterbalance the ring's memory of being twisted open the opposite way. *Slowly*, release your right-hand pliers' pressure, and the right side should snap into place with an audible click.

7 When the ring is closed properly, the closed edges are flush and the ring is even on both sides of the cut edges. Notice that the gaps between the jaws of the pliers line up, as shown, when the ring is properly closed. When working with shiny silver rings, looking for even, lined-up gaps can be an easier way to check for proper closure than checking the flush ends of the ring.

Spiraling Rings and Flower Formations

This practice exercise will help you perfect your techniques for spiraling rings into Flower formations, used in many of the projects in this book.

Bottomwise Spiraling Technique

For consistent spiraling, always twist open each ring the exact same way (see Working with Jump Rings, page 26). **For right-handers:** Hold the right side of the open ring with the right-hand pliers and feed the left tip of the ring *counterclockwise*, from the *bottom* up through the center of the previous ring. **For left-handers:** Hold the left side of the open ring with the left-hand pliers and feed the right tip of the ring *clockwise*, from the *bottom* up through the center of the previous ring.

Note: The following photographs illustrate the right-handed technique.

Tools: Two flat-nose pliers.

Materials: Four 14-gauge, 7mm ID jump rings (one each in silver, gold, bronze, and copper). Feel free to use any size jump rings (wrapped according to the Flower aspect ratio of 4.3), but larger rings are easier to learn with.

1 With the first (copper) ring closed, add the second (silver) ring using the bottomwise technique above. Close the second ring.

2 Add the third (gold) ring the same way you added the second ring; close the gold ring flush. For a four-ring Flower, add and close the fourth (bronze) ring as you did the second and third rings.

LEFT SIDE HIGH

After you've completed your three- or four-ring Flower, look inward on the Flower and make sure the *left* side of each ring is high (if you are right-handed). For left-handers, you will end up with a *right-side-high* spiral. Either way is fine; just make sure all your rings are spiraling at the same angle.

Note: We refer to this technique as "left side high" throughout the book.

FORGING AN S-CLASP

When I started making chain, I could not find a sturdy and reliable clasping system that also aesthetically complemented my jewelry designs. Necessity being the mother of invention, I put a hammer to anvil for quite a while to "bang" out this signature S-clasp design. Many of the necklace and bracelet projects in this book are finished with an S-clasp (made from forged, S-shaped 14-gauge wire) at one end of the chain that fastens through a catch ring at the other end.

Tools: Planishing hammer, steel anvil, mandrel-tip pliers (3.1mm) or round-nose pliers (marked at a 3.1mm diameter), side cutters, flat file, superfine sanding pad, and measuring tape.

Materials: One 1¾-inch-long, 14-gauge silver wire and three 14-gauge, 5.5mm ID silver jump rings (one attaches the S-clasp to the chain, two are assembled 1+1 as adjustable catch rings).

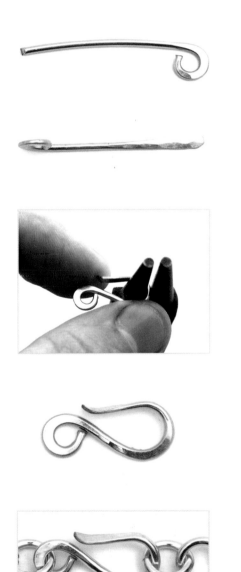

1 Using side cutters, cut a 1¾-inch length of 14-gauge wire; one end will have a burr, the other will be flat. Use the mandrel-tip pliers' 3.1mm jaw to bend ½ inch of the flat end of the wire into a small single loop. Place the wire on the anvil and gently forge (flatten) the small loop with the hammer. The small loop will open slightly when it is forged; close this gap by squeezing with the flat-nose pliers, keeping the tips of the pliers flat against the anvil surface.

2 Forge the burr end of the wire into a tapered tongue shape—about half the remaining wire length. Use a flat file to shape the wire's tip and sanding pad to round it smoothly. Bend the tip of the flattened wire 45 degrees upward to create a "ski tip" to serve as the catch ring's gateway.

3 Using round-nose pliers (marked at 6.3mm diameter), grip the wire halfway between the ski tip and small loop and bend both ends of the wire toward one another equally till the bottom of the ski tip is touching the small loop.

4 Lay the wire on the anvil and forge the remaining round wire, leaving the wire thicker toward both the small loop and the ski tip of the tongue. Straighten the clasp with pliers as necessary, and adjust the large loop as needed to allow passage of the 14-gauge catch ring.

5 Connect the small loop of the clasp to one end of the chain with a single 14-gauge jump ring. Add the 1+1 jump ring connection to the opposite end of the chain to serve as the catch rings. Thread the large loop of the clasp through either catch ring for an adjustable-length closure to any bracelet or necklace.

SINGLE-LOOP-AROUND BEAD SETTING

The single-loop-around bead setting technique allows a gemstone bead to be held between the headpin's ball and the single loop of wire beyond the bead, securing the tail end of the wire by wrapping it around the base wire between the single loop and the bead.

Use 1½-inch headpins to set beads of varying sizes with the following techniques: Set beads up to 15mm in length with the single-loop-around technique, set beads up to 10mm in length with the double-loop technique (see page 36), and set beads up to 4mm in length with the triple-loop-around technique (see page 40).

Tools: Mandrel-tip pliers (3.1mm) or round-nose pliers (marked at 3.1mm diameter), chain-nose pliers, side cutters, measuring tape, and a felt-tip marker.

Materials: One or more 1½-inch-long, 19-gauge headpin(s), and one or more 4mm diameter by 13mm long tube bead(s).

Note: To make your own headpins, see page 154.

1 Add a tube bead to a 1½-inch silver headpin. Using measuring tape and a felt-tip marker, mark the silver wire at ½ inch beyond the bead.

2 Using mandrel-tip pliers, grip the wire at the mark, keeping the 3.1mm mandrel jaw toward you.

3 Keeping finger pressure where the wire is bending, slowly bend the wire between the mark and bead upward and around the 3.1mm jaw, until the wires cross, laying the bead to the right (toward the tool) of the wire tail.

4 Looking down on the mandrel-tip pliers and using chain-nose pliers (Steps 4–6), grip the ½-inch wire tail.

5 Bend the ½-inch wire tail downward and around the 19-gauge base wire until it touches the single loop.

6 Bend the carnelian tube 30 degrees backward so that it comes from the aesthetic center of the single loop. Re-grip the wire tail with the chain-nose pliers and bend it upward and around the 19-gauge base wire, completing a 360-degree loop-around, as shown.

7 Using side cutters, trim off the excess wire and straighten the single-loop-around as needed to complete the bead setting. Put your fingers over the excess wire to keep it from flying across the room.

Practice, practice, practice—getting consistency with wire manipulation takes time and patience.

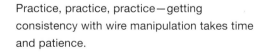

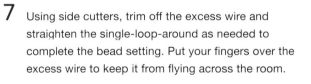

BEADED SINGLE-CHAIN BRACELET AND EARRINGS

The Beaded Single-Chain Bracelet is assembled as a simple one-on-one chain with a single-loop-around bead setting added onto every other jump ring in repetitive pattern, creating a fringe of gemstone beads from the Single chain. This simple jewelry pattern illustrates many of the key concepts of beaded chain that are expanded upon throughout this book.

Tools: Two flat-nose pliers, mandrel-tip pliers (3.1mm) or round-nose pliers (marked at 3.1mm diameter), chain-nose pliers, side cutters, measuring tape, and a felt-tip marker.

Materials for bracelet: Sixty-one 16-gauge, 2.75mm ID bronze jump rings; three 15-gauge, 5mm ID bronze catch rings; thirty 1½-inch-long, 19-gauge silver headpins; thirty 4mm diameter x 13mm long red carnelian tube beads; and one bronze S-clasp, for an 8-inch bracelet.

Materials for earrings: Twelve 16-gauge, 2.75mm ID bronze jump rings; two 2-inch-long, 19-gauge silver headpins for earring backs; six 1½-inch-long, 19-gauge silver headpins for bead setting; and six 4mm diameter x 13mm long red carnelian tube beads.

Note: To make your own headpins, see page 154.

1 Set all thirty beads onto the headpins using the single-loop-around technique (see page 30). Starting with a paperclip to signify a beginning point, assemble (1+1) two 16-gauge rings, then add the first single-loop-around bead setting onto the second jump ring, as shown.

2 Assemble (1+1) the next two 16-gauge rings, then add a second single-loop-around bead setting onto the fourth jump ring, as shown.

3 Continue this pattern, assembling a Single (1+1) chain of 16-gauge rings, adding a bead setting onto every other (even) ring so they all hang on one side of the Single chain. Add a bronze S-clasp and catch rings (see page 29) to finish the bracelet.

To make the Beaded Single-Chain Earrings, create six single-loop-around bead settings (see page 30) using 1½-inch silver headpins and 4mm × 13mm carnelian tube beads. For each earring, use six 16-gauge, 2.75mm bronze rings, assembled 1+1+1 (see page 24), adding a bead setting to every other ring.

BENDING MATCHING EARRING BACKS

The principle behind a matching pair of earring backs is to bend both headpin wires at the same time around a single mandrel, so that both earring backs will be identically shaped.

Tools: Two flat-nose pliers; mandrel-tip pliers (3.1mm); round-nose pliers (marked at 2.5mm and 3.1mm diameter); chain-nose pliers; side cutters; two bending mandrels, one small (2.35mm) and one large (8mm); measuring tape; and felt-tip marker.

Materials: Two 2-inch-long, 19-gauge silver headpins.

Note: A 2.35mm steel mandrel is available at your hardware store as a 3/32-inch rod, typically sold in 3-foot lengths; you'll need a 5-inch length. Use an 8mm plastic mechanical pencil for the large mandrel. If you can't find one, look in your hardware store for a 5/16-inch steel rod or wooden dowel.

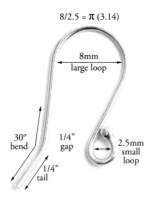

$8/2.5 = \pi \ (3.14)$

8mm large loop

30° bend

1/4" gap

2.5mm small loop

1/4" tail

This diagram illustrates all the details of the earring backs design. Starting at the end of the headpin with a soldered-on 2mm ball, bend a 2.5mm small loop around the 2.5mm jaw of the round-nose pliers. Next, bend the wire around a 8mm mandrel to form the large loop. As the large loop is being formed, the tip of the wire will come down past the small loop by a quarter of an inch; bend it outward by 30 degrees at this point. The large and small loops are in harmonious balance because they are in a proportion of pi (Π) = 3.14.

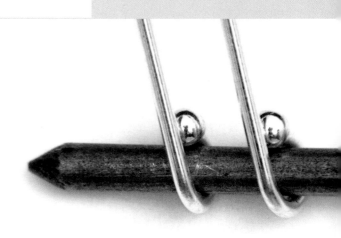

1 Using digital calipers and a fine-point felt-tip marker, mark the jaws of your round-nose pliers at 2.5mm. Grip the headpin below the ball and bend the wire up around the round-nose jaw at the 2.5mm mark in a complete loop. Repeat on a second 2-inch headpin.

2 Add both small loops, facing the same way, onto the 2.35mm (steel rod) mandrel.

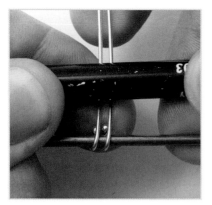

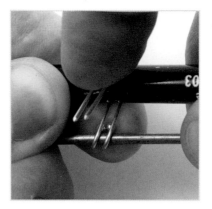

3 With the 2.35mm steel rod holding both wires, place the 8mm pencil mandrel in front of the wires, keeping both mandrels parallel and spaced about 8mm apart.

4 Keeping both mandrels parallel and maintaining the gap between the wires, simultaneously bend both wires over the large mandrel. While bending, allow the wire tips to travel past their small loops by a quarter of an inch, creating a tail that will help counterbalance the weight of the earring design.

5 Remove both wires from the mandrel and grip both ¼-inch wire tails with flat-nose pliers simultaneously. Bend both wires in a slight (30-degree) outward bend. This bend creates a safety stop to prevent loss of the earring.

6 The finished earring back may need a pinch of straightening. Using flat-nose pliers, grip the small loop, look down on the wire, and adjust the form as needed.

Adding Earring Designs to Earring Backs

7 To add bead settings to earring backs, twist open the small loop of the back just like a jump ring, add your earring design, and twist the small loop closed.

DOUBLE-LOOP BEAD SETTING

The double-loop bead-setting technique allows a gemstone bead to be securely held between the headpin's ball and the double loop of wire beyond the bead.

Tools: Round-nose pliers (marked at a 2.5mm diameter) and side cutters, measuring tape, and felt-tip marker.

Materials: One or more 1¼-inch-long, 20-gauge headpin(s), and one or more 4mm round bead(s).

Note: To make your own headpins, see page 154.

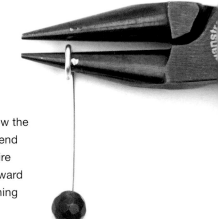

1 Add a 4mm amethyst bead onto one headpin. There will be just over an inch of wire beyond the bead, which you will need to complete a full double loop.

2 Using round-nose plies (Steps 2–6), grip the end of the 20-gauge headpin wire and bend the wire upward and around the 2.5mm jaw, stopping before the wire goes over the next jaw.

3 Release the jaw pressure and allow the bead and balled end of the headpin wire to rotate back toward you to the beginning position.

4 Re-grip the wire with the pliers, keeping your finger pressure where the wire is bending, and bring the headpin wire upward, laying it to the right of the previously wrapped wire and wrapping inward toward the tool in a tight coil, stopping before the wire goes over the next jaw.

5 Release the jaw pressure and allow the bead and balled end to rotate back toward you to the beginning position. Re-grip the wire with the pliers and bend the headpin wire upward, laying the new wire to the right of the previously wrapped wire and stopping before the wire goes over the next jaw.

6 Release the jaw pressure and allow the bead and balled end to rotate back toward you to the beginning position. Re-grip the loops with the pliers and bend the remaining wire to bring the bead snug against the double loop.

7 With the 20-gauge wire-wrapped loops snug against the bead, notice that the wire actually travels two and a quarter times around the mandrel. Using side cutters, trim off the excess wire beyond a full two rotations at a 45-degree angle.

It takes time and patience to be consistent in your wire wrapping, and you'll need to practice this technique to get there. This bead-setting technique will be used in the Namaste Tripoli Bracelet on page 76.

DOUBLE-LOOP-AROUND MAGNETIC CLASP

The double-loop-around bead-setting technique allows a gemstone bead, or in this case a stack of magnetic disk beads, to be held between the headpin's ball and the double loop of wire beyond the bead, securing the tail end of the wire by wrapping it around the base wire between the double loop and the bead. The double-loop-around technique has a couple advantages over the more simplified double-loop technique (page 36)—aesthetically it allows the bead to hang straight down from the double loop, and it is a much stronger wire setting that cannot be easily unraveled.

I designed this magnetic clasp to assist my late grandmothers who found the S-clasp difficult to maneuver. This unique clasping system is based on wire-setting two groups of magnetic beads so that they have attracting magnetic polarity. Each group consists of two or more disk-shaped magnetic beads that are stacked up against the headpin's ball and double-looped to set them. Take care which way you start the headpin through the bead group; the bead settings must have attracting polarity so that the balled ends of the headpins attract each other and the double loops are facing outward. Finally, a single magnetic tube-shaped bead is used between the bead settings to cover both headpin balls.

1 Add the first group of three magnetic beads onto one 19-gauge headpin. Place a second group of three magnetic beads next to the first group (on the headpin) so their sides attract, then place the second headpin through this second group.

2 If the bead groups are in proper magnetic attraction, the groups are attracted to each other, with the headpins' balls inward.

3 You will have roughly 1 ³/₈ inch of 19-gauge wire beyond the three magnetic beads. Using a fine-point felt-tip marker, mark the wire at 1 inch beyond the beads, leaving ³/₈ inch from this mark to the wire tip.

Tools: Mandrel-tip pliers (3.1mm) or round-nose pliers (marked at a 3.1mm diameter), chain-nose pliers, side cutters, measuring tape, and a felt-tip marker.

Materials: Two 19-gauge, 1½-inch headpins; six 6mm diameter × 1mm thick (disk) magnetic beads; and one 6mm diameter x 4mm long (tube) magnetic bead.

Note: To make your own headpins, see page 154.

4 **Far left:** Using mandrel-tip pliers, grip the wire at the pen mark, keeping the 3.1mm-sized mandrel toward you. Bend the 1 inch of headpin wire upward around the 3.1mm mandrel jaw, coiling toward the right of the wire tail and stopping before the wire goes over the next (3.9mm) jaw, as shown.

5 **Middle left:** Relax your grip on the pliers, allowing the beaded headpin to rotate backward toward the beginning position. Re-grip the wire with the pliers and again bend the headpin wire upward around the 3.1mm mandrel jaw, coiling right, as you did in Step 4.

6 **Middle right:** Relax your grip on the pliers, allowing the beaded headpin to rotate backward toward the beginning position. Re-grip the wire with the pliers and bend the headpin wire upward in a tight coil till the wires overlap and the double loop is snug against the magnetic bead group.

7 **Far right:** Note that the photographs for Steps 7–11 are shot looking down on the tips of the mandrel-tipped pliers. Using the chain-nose pliers (for Steps 7–11), grip the tip of the wire tail of the headpin and bend it downward.

8 **Far left:** Bring the wire tail 180 degrees around the 19-gauge wire, like a neck scarf, between the double loop and the bead group.

9 **Middle left:** Grip the headpin's ball and bend the magnetic beads 30 degrees backward so that the beads hang directly under the double loop.

10 **Middle right:** Re-grip the headpin's wire tail and bend it upward around the 19-gauge wire between the double loop and magnetic beads.

11 **Far right:** Use the tips of the chain-nose pliers to finish the wire tail as it completes a full 360-degree wrap around. Use the side cutters to trim off any excess wire. Repeat Steps 3–11 to set the second magnetic bead group. Combine both bead settings with the center tube-shaped magnetic bead to complete the clasp.

TRIPLE-LOOP-AROUND CRYSTAL SETTING

The triple-loop-around crystal setting allows an amethyst crystal to be held between the headpin's ball and the triple loop of wire beyond the crystal, securing the tail end of the wire by wrapping it around the base wire between the triple loop and the crystal. The triple-loop-around crystal will be used on the Crystal Triangle Earrings on page 84.

Tools: Round-nose pliers (marked at a 2.5mm diameter), chain-nose pliers, side cutters, measuring tape, and a felt-tip marker.

Materials: Two 2¾-inch-long, 20-gauge silver headpins; two 8mm diameter × 22mm long amethyst crystals that have been predrilled to be strung lengthwise.

Note: To make your own headpins, see page 154.

1 Find two matching amethyst crystals and add one each onto the two 20-gauge headpins.

2 You will have roughly 1¾ inch of 20-gauge wire beyond the crystal. Using a fine-point felt-tip marker, mark the wire at 1³/₈ inch beyond the crystal, leaving ³/₈ inch from this mark to the wire tip.

3 Using the round-nose pliers (for Steps 3–5), grip the wire at the pen mark, and at the marked diameter on the pliers, bend the 1³/₈ inch of headpin wire (between the mark and the crystal) upward around the jaw, coiling toward the right of the wire tail and stopping before the wire goes over the next jaw, as shown.

4 Relax your grip on the pliers, allowing the crystal headpin to rotate backward toward the beginning position. Re-grip the wire with the pliers and bend the headpin wire upward around the marked diameter jaw, coiling toward the right of the wire tail and stopping before the wire goes over the next jaw, as shown.

5 Relax your grip on the pliers, allowing the crystal headpin to rotate backward toward the beginning position. Re-grip the wire with the pliers and bend the headpin wire upward in a tight coil till the wires overlap and the triple loop is snug against the crystal.

6 Note that the photographs for Steps 6–11 are shot looking down on the tips of the round-nose pliers. Using chain-nose pliers (Steps 6–10), grip the tip of the ³/₈-inch wire tail of the headpin and bend it downward.

7 Bring the wire tail 180 degrees around the 20-gauge wire, like a neck scarf between the triple loop and crystal.

8 Grip the headpin's ball and bend the crystal 30 degrees backward so that the crystal hangs directly under the triple loop.

9 Re-grip the headpin's wire tail and bend it upward around the 20-gauge wire between the triple loop and crystal.

10 Use the tips of the chain-nose pliers to finish the wire tail as it completes a full 360-degree wrap around, as shown. Use the side cutters to trim off any excess wire.

11 The finished crystal setting with a triple-loop-around technique. Repeat Steps 2–11 to set the second crystal. (See page 84 for the Crystal Triangle Earrings, which use this bead setting.)

3 The Byzantine Revisited

This chapter presents the basics of the Byzantine chain and how it can be used in a variety of ways, the three most common mistakes in Byzantine chain making (and how to avoid them), and how to connect two Byzantine chain lengths. We begin by assembling a few lengths of Byzantine chain to make the Byzantine Earrings, Key Fob, and Bracelet—each project using a different gauge of wire jump rings. We show how to set beads into the Byzantine sections and then add Flower spirals for the Beaded Romanov Bracelet and Earrings. We make the Serrated Byzantine Earrings and Bracelet from small lengths of Byzantine chain, which are offset by a length of large rings down the middle. Finally, we assemble multiple Byzantine chain sections into the Triple Byzantine Key Fob and add a triplet of beads to the terminating end.

ASSEMBLING THE BYZANTINE CHAIN

The Byzantine chain is an age-old pattern that has been known by many different names. During the Renaissance, it was a court artisan's secret, known as the King's Braid. In the movie Braveheart, Mel Gibson wears a sash of three Byzantine chains across his chest, showing his nobility. It has also been know as the Sequential Link Idiot's Delight and the Birdcage and is very similar to the Bali chain that hails from the Pacific island of the same name.

The Byzantine chain is used in projects throughout the book—from small sections to necklace chain lengths and as components the Tripoli, Clover, and Snowflake formations. You need to stay focused when assembling the Byzantine chain, particularly when you get a few inches into it and think, "I've got this down. I can watch some TV while I work." There are a few common mistakes that can sneak up on you that we discuss on page 45.

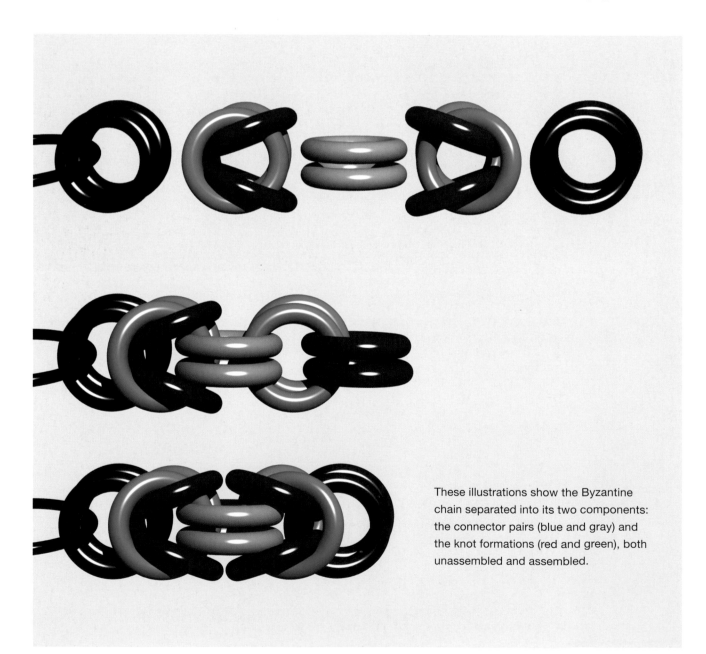

These illustrations show the Byzantine chain separated into its two components: the connector pairs (blue and gray) and the knot formations (red and green), both unassembled and assembled.

Here are three very common mistakes that almost all beginners make (more than once) before mastering the Byzantine chain pattern. Counting to six will help, but you will also need to memorize the visual key of the 2+2+2 pattern and know when to fold back the knot formation to add the next connector pair, to avoid these mistakes.

#1 Most Common Mistake:
Adding Two Pairs (2+2) Instead of Three Pairs (2+2+2)

If you mistakenly add only two pairs (2+2), instead of the requisite three pairs (2+2+2), the folded-back knot formation will be too tight against the previous knot formation.

When you fold back this 2+2 pattern, it will cause the outer rings to stick out of the chain. Adding two connector rings through this too-tight knot formation is very difficult, and the pattern cannot be continued.

#2 Most Common Mistake:
Connector Pair Travels in Wrong Direction Through Knot Formation

The Byzantine chain ends correctly in a 2+2+2 pattern; the mistake is that the added connector pair travels perpendicularly through the knot formation.

Because the added connector pair mistakenly travels perpendicularly through the knot formation, it is added only to the inner silver pair of the knot, leaving the outer silver pair to flop about.

#3 Most Common Mistake:
Adding Four Pair (2+2+2+2) Instead of Three Pair (2+2+2)

If you mistakenly add four pair (2+2+2+2) instead of three pair (2+2+2), there will be an extra connector pair between the knot formations.

When you fold back this 2+2+2+2 pattern, you'll notice an aesthetic gap in the chain patterns.

BYZANTINE EARRINGS
AND KEY FOB

To put theory into practice, let's start
assembling the Byzantine chain with some
very large 15-gauge silver and bronze jump
rings into two chain lengths that will be
suspended by earring backs.

Tools: Two flat-nose pliers, one paperclip, and a
length of scrap wire to hold rings open.

Materials for earrings: Twelve 15-gauge, 5mm
bronze jump rings; sixteen 15-gauge, 5mm silver
jump rings; and two 19-gauge, 2-inch-long silver
headpins for earring backs.

Materials for key fob: Ten 15-gauge, 5mm
bronze jump rings; sixteen 15-gauge, 5mm silver
jump rings; and a key ring.

Note: To make your own headpins, see page 154.

Byzantine Earrings

2 Fold back the outer silver pair and angle open the inner silver pair into the first knot formation, holding it open with a scrap wire.

1 Start with a paperclip, to signify a beginning point, and add two 15-gauge bronze rings as the first connector pair. Add four 15-gauge silver rings (two pair), assembled 2+2 onto the previous bronze pair, creating a 2+2+2 pattern.

3 Add two 15-gauge bronze rings through the knot formation as the second connector pair.

4 Add four 15-gauge silver rings (two pair), assembled 2+2 onto the previous bronze pair, creating a 2+2+2 pattern.

5 Fold back the outer silver pair and angle open the inner silver pair into the second knot formation, held open with a scrap wire.

6 Add two 15-gauge bronze rings through the knot formation as the third connector pair.

7 Remove the paperclip and add the small loop of the earring back (see page 34) through the beginning bronze pair of rings. Repeat Steps 1–7 to make a matching pair of earrings.

Byzantine Key Fob

If your earlobes are not pierced, no worries, mate; you can follow the instructions above to make a masculine key fob. Follow Steps 1-7, but make one Byzantine chain length, not two, and, in Step 7, add the key fob ring instead of the earring back.

BYZANTINE BRACELET

Once we have made a bit of the Byzantine chain in the larger 15-gauge size rings, let's work with a smaller 17-gauge ring size to craft a full bracelet. The smaller jump rings will make a thinner chain that is more suitable for a bracelet. Smaller rings also mean more links per inch and thus require more attention to detail.

Tools: Flat-nose pliers, one paperclip, and a length of scrap wire to hold rings open.

Materials: Fifty-two 17-gauge, 4mm ID bronze jump rings; one hundred 17-gauge, 4mm ID silver jump rings; three 15-gauge, 5mm ID silver jump rings; and a silver S-clasp, for an 8-inch bracelet.

1 Following Steps 1–6 of the Byzantine Earrings (see page 46), assemble the first two knot formations of the bracelet chain length, alternating bronze and silver ring pairs as shown.

2 Add four 17-gauge silver rings (two pair), assembled 2+2 onto the ending bronze connector pair of the second knot formation, creating a 2+2+2 pattern.

3 Fold back and angle open the silver pairs into the third knot formation, holding it open with a scrap wire; add two 17-gauge bronze rings through the knot formation as the fourth connector pair.

4 Add four 17-gauge silver rings (two pair), assembled 2+2 onto the previous bronze pair, creating a 2+2+2 pattern.

5 Fold back and angle open the silver pairs into the fourth knot formation, holding it open with a scrap wire; add two 17-gauge bronze rings through the knot formation as the fifth connector pair. You now have a complete Byzantine pattern.

6 Continue assembling the Byzantine chain pattern into a 7-inch length. Add the silver S-clasp and catch rings (see page 29) to make an 8-inch bracelet.

CONNECTING BYZANTINE CHAINS

The Byzantine chain is unique because it is a sequential chain with a connector pair between each knot formation, which allows the two chain sections to be easily spliced together into a continuous chain length by adding a connector pair of rings between two knot formations.

1 **Left:** Both Byzantine chain lengths will need to terminate in a 2+2+2 chain pattern to allow the ending knot formation to be folded back and angled open, as shown (held open with scrap wires).

2 **Right:** Using chain-nose pliers, add the first connector ring (shown in bronze) through the rectangular opening within both (silver) knot formations. Use the tips of the chain-nose pliers to close this first connector ring.

3 **Left:** Add the second connector ring (shown in bronze), parallel to the first connector ring, through both knot formations.

4 **Right:** Use the tips of the chain-nose pliers to close the second connector ring. Take care that both wire ends are brought into flush alignment without a gap.

BEADED ROMANOV BRACELET AND EARRINGS

The Beaded Romanov Bracelet
starts with the bead setting by
bending the wire into a double-loop
on both sides of the 6mm bead.
The silver Byzantine chain is then
assembled from these double loops
and combined at both ends with a
three-ring spiraling bronze Large
Flower formation (see page 28), to
give color and aesthetic dimension to
this dynamic beaded-chain bracelet
project. As a variation of this beaded
bracelet design, you can make
matching earrings.

Tools: Two flat-nose pliers, chain-nose
pliers (optional), mandrel-tip (3.5mm) or
round-nose pliers (marked at a 3.5mm
diameter), side cutters, and a length of
scrap wire.

Materials for 8-inch bracelet: Eight
18-gauge, 2¾-inch-long silver wires;
one hundred ninety-two 18-gauge,
3.5mm ID silver jump rings; twenty-
seven 17-gauge, 8.75mm ID gold jump
rings; two 15-gauge, 5mm ID catch
rings; eight 6mm red carnelian beads;
and a silver S-clasp.

Materials for earrings: Two 18-gauge,
2¾-inch-long silver wires; forty-eight
18-gauge, 3.5mm ID silver jump rings;
twelve 17-gauge, 8.75mm gold jump
rings; eight 6mm red carnelian beads;
and two 19-gauge, 2-inch silver
headpins for earring backs.

Note: To make your own headpins, see
page 154.

Beaded Romanov Bracelet

1 Cut 18-gauge silver wire into eight 2¾-inch lengths. Wrap a double loop (see page 36) with the 3.5mm jaw, add a 6mm red carnelian bead, and wrap a second double loop in an opposite spiral to encase the bead. Add eight 18-gauge rings (shown in copper), four onto each double loop, as shown.

2 Add eight 18-gauge rings (shown in copper), two onto each pair added in Step 1, creating four 2+2 patterns, to be folded back and angled open into four knot formations.

3 Add eight 18-gauge, rings (shown in copper), two through each of the four folded-back and angled-open knot formations, to complete both Byzantine chain sections with an ending connector pair of rings. Repeat Steps 1–3 seven more times, creating eight beaded chain formations.

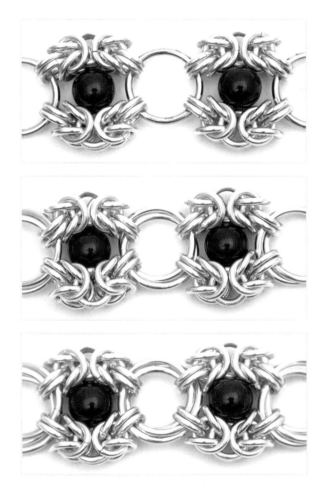

4 **Top:** Add nine 17-gauge gold rings (shown in copper), one between each beaded chain formation, traveling through the ending connector pair (added in Step 3) of each Byzantine chain section.

5 **Middle:** Add nine 17-gauge gold rings, each spiraling around the first gold ring added in Step 4, creating a two-ring spiral Flower formation (see page 28) between each beaded Byzantine section.

6 **Bottom:** Add nine 17-gauge gold rings, each spiraling around the first and second gold rings, creating a three-ring spiral Flower formation between each beaded Byzantine section. Add the silver S-clasp and catch rings (see page 29) to finish the bracelet.

Beaded Romanov Earrings

The Beaded Romanov Earrings are created by following Steps 1–3 of the above Byzantine Bracelet to assemble two beaded Byzantine chain sections. Spiral twelve 17-gauge rings as four three-ring Large Flower formations (see page 28), one on each end of the two beaded chain sections. Add earring backs (see page 34) to the Large Flower formation for a matching pair of earrings.

SERRATED BYZANTINE EARRINGS AND BRACELET

The Serrated Byzantine Earring and Bracelet projects allow small sections of gold Byzantine chain to be assembled in an offset pattern on both sides of a simple 1+2+1 chain pattern. The 1+2+1 chain is assembled with single large silver rings connected with pairs of copper rings to create a copper stripe down the center of the chain. The offset pattern of the gold Byzantine chain sections causes them to bend around each of the single silver rings, so the overall chain edge undulates in a scalloping pattern, similar to a serrated chef's knife.

Tools: Flat-nose pliers.

Materials for earrings: Eight 15-gauge, 5mm silver jump rings; sixty-eight 19-gauge, 3.1mm jump rings (twelve copper and fifty-six gold); and two 19-gauge, 2-inch silver headpins for the earring backs.

Materials for bracelet: Twenty-two 15-gauge, 5mm silver jump rings; forty-two 19-gauge, 3.1mm copper jump rings; two hundred eighty 19-gauge, 3.1mm gold rings; and a golden magnetic clasp to make an 8-inch bracelet.

Note: To make your own headpins, see page 154.

Serrated Byzantine Earrings

1   Start with ten 19-gauge, 3.1mm gold jump rings, assembled in five pairs, in a 2+2+2+2+2 pattern.

2   Fold back and angle open the knot formation on the left and add two 19-gauge gold rings (shown in copper) through the knot formation.

3   Fold back and angle open the knot formation on the right and add two 19-gauge gold rings (shown in copper) through the knot formation. Repeat Steps 1–3 to create a second Byzantine chain section, fourteen gold rings in volume.

1st   2nd   3rd   4th

4   Assemble four 15-gauge silver rings with three pair of 19-gauge copper rings between in a 1+2+1+2+1+2+1 pattern, as shown.

5   **Top:** Open the first silver ring and add the two beginning rings of the first gold Byzantine chain section.

6   **Bottom:** Open the third silver ring and add the opposite two ending rings of the first gold Byzantine chain section (added to the first silver ring in Step 5).

7 Open the second silver ring and add the two beginning rings of the second gold Byzantine chain section.

1 Refer to Steps 1–8 of the Serrated Byzantine Earrings (page 55). Follow Steps 1–3, making twenty Byzantine chain sections, each fourteen rings in volume. Follow Step 4 to assemble the 1+2+1 pattern of twenty-two 15-gauge silver rings with two 19-gauge copper rings between until the pattern is 7 inches long. Follow Steps 5–8, adding the Byzantine chain sections to the 15-gauge silver rings.

8 Open the fourth silver ring and add the opposite two ending rings of the second gold Byzantine chain section (added to the second silver ring in Step 7).

9 Add the small loop of the earring back (see page 34) through the ending 15-gauge silver ring. Repeat Steps 1–9 to make a matching pair of earrings.

2 Once you have a 7-inch-long Serrated Byzantine chain pattern, add the golden magnetic clasp to the ends of the chain (see page 38), to complete an 8-inch bracelet.

TRIPLE BYZANTINE
KEY FOB

The Triple Byzantine Key Fob combines three small sections of Byzantine chain into an intricate round chain pattern. We will work with very small 20-gauge silver jump rings to assemble the Byzantine chain sections. Single 16-gauge rings will connect pairs of these chain sections, and a third Byzantine chain section will be built into the chain. The end of the key fob is embellished with three 8mm faceted blue quartz beads set onto headpins with a double loop.

Tools: Two flat-nose pliers, two chain-nose pliers, mandrel-tip pliers (3.1mm), round-nose pliers (marked at 3.1mm in diameter), side cutters, and two lengths of scrap wire to hold rings open.

Materials: One hundred twenty-six 20-gauge, 2.75mm ID silver jump rings; four 16-gauge, 4.5mm ID silver jump rings; three 1½-inch-long, 19-gauge silver headpins; three 8mm faceted blue quartz beads; and a key ring.

Note: If you find that 20-gauge jump rings are too small for you, try 19-gauge, 3.1mm rings for the Byzantine chain and 15-gauge, 5mm rings for the connectors, or 18-gauge, 3.5mm for the Byzantine and 14-gauge, 5.5mm for the connectors.

Note: To make your own headpins, see page 154.

1 Using the 3.1mm jaw of the mandrel-tip pliers and three headpins, create double-loop bead settings (see page 36) for each of the three blue quartz beads. Start the chain pattern by assembling seven Byzantine chain sections (see page 44), each consisting of fourteen 20-gauge rings. Connect three Byzantine chain sections with one 16-gauge ring (shown in brass).

2 Stack the three (silver) Byzantine chain sections so the 16-gauge (silver) ring is vertical. Add a second 16-gauge ring (shown in brass) through the ending rings of the previous three Byzantine sections and add two more Byzantine sections (shown in gold). Be sure to alternate the previous (silver) Byzantine sections and the newly added (gold) Byzantine sections, as shown.

3 Add a third 16-gauge ring (shown in brass) through the ending rings of the previous two Byzantine sections and add two more Byzantine sections (shown in gold). Be sure to alternate the previous (silver) Byzantine sections and the newly added (gold) Byzantine sections.

4 Add a fourth 16-gauge ring (shown in brass) through the ending rings of the previous two Byzantine sections and add three double loops of the 8mm bead settings. Be sure to alternate the previous Byzantine sections and the newly added double loops, keeping all the double-loop spirals in the same outward-angling direction.

5 To build the third Byzantine chain section into the second column created in Step 2, add two six-ring 2+2+2 chain patterns (shown in gold) onto the 16-gauge vertical rings on both sides of the second column.

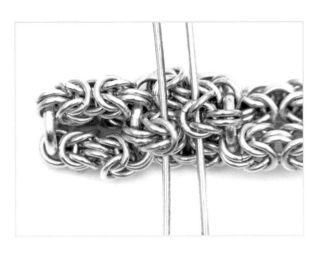

6 Fold back and angle open both knot formations, holding each open with a scrap wire, as shown.

7 Connect both knot formations (shown in gold) with a pair of 20-gauge rings (shown in copper) to complete the third Byzantine chain section of the second column (see Connecting Byzantine Chains on page 49).

8 To build the third Byzantine chain section into the third column, add two six-ring 2+2+2 chain patterns (shown in gold) onto the 16-gauge vertical rings on both sides of the third column.

9 Fold back and angle open both knot formations, just as you did in Step 6. Connect both knot formations with a pair of 20-gauge rings (shown in copper). Add the split key ring to the beginning 16-gauge ring of the chain length to complete the Triple Byzantine Key Fob.

4 Tripoli Formations

This chapter illustrates how to assemble the Tripoli formation, a Byzantine chain derivative that features three knot formations radiating from the center connector pair. The Tripoli's three-way connection is the basis for most of the beaded chain designs in this book. We first practice this technique with large rings and then add beads to the form to make the Beaded Tripoli (9) Earrings and the Beaded Tripoli (3) Bracelet. We get a bit more sophisticated with the Jens Pind Beaded Tripoli Bracelet, which balances two beaded Tripoli forms between two lengths of tri-metal Jens Pind chain. In the Suspended Tripoli Bracelet, the Tripoli formations are built from double-loop-around bead settings, which are then suspended from a simple 1+2+1 chain. Finally, the Namaste Tripoli Bracelet uses double-loop beaded Tripolis on both sides of a folded-back chain for an amazing bracelet pattern like no other.

ASSEMBLING THE TRIPOLI FORMATION

The Tripoli is a unique derivative of the ancient Byzantine chain, but instead of it being a linear chain, three knot formations radiate from the center pair of rings, and all three points terminate with an ending pair of rings. We start by assembling a small section of the Byzantine chain and then add the third knot formation (silver), assembled 2+2, from the center pair of (copper) rings. This third knot formation is folded back and completed with an ending pair of (bronze) rings.

Assembling the Tripoli from Byzantine Chain

Tools: Two flat-nose pliers and a length of scrap wire to hold rings open.

Materials: Twenty 15-gauge, 5mm ID jump rings (two copper, twelve silver, six bronze), and a split key ring (optional).

1 Start by joining ten rings, two copper and eight silver, assembled 2+2+2+2+2. Note that the two center rings are copper to signify the center of the Tripoli formation.

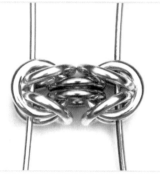

2 On both sides of the chain formation, fold back the four silver rings and angle them open into knot formations, revealing the rectangular opening within the Byzantine chain pattern. Hold each knot formation open with a scrap wire, as shown.

3 Add two bronze rings through the knot formation on the left. Add two bronze rings through the knot formation on the right, creating a Byzantine chain section.

4 Add four silver rings, assembled 2+2, to the center copper pair of rings, as shown.

5 Fold back and angle open the third knot formation. Notice that it will hold itself open if you tuck the folded-back rings under the previously folded-back rings of the first and second knot formations.

6 Add two bronze rings through the third knot formation to complete the Tripoli formation.

Assembling the Tripoli from the Center

In the last section, we assembled the Tripoli formation from a Byzantine chain section. A simplified solution for mass production is to assemble the Tripoli from the center outwardly. Starting with the center pair of (copper) rings, we add on the three (silver) knot formations and complete each of the three knots with an ending pair of (bronze) rings.

Tools: Two flat-nose pliers.

Materials: Twenty 18-gauge, 3.5mm ID jump rings (two copper, twelve silver, and six bronze).

1 Start by opening one copper ring and adding five silver rings. Note that you do not have to open each silver ring to add it into the chain pattern individually. Close all rings.

2 Add one copper ring, parallel to the first copper ring, through the five silver rings.

3 Add the sixth silver ring so that you have six silver rings radiating from two copper rings.

4 Add six silver rings, two to each pair of silver rings added in Step 3.

5 Fold back and angle open the top (twelve o'clock) silver knot formation and add two bronze rings.

6 Fold back and angle open the right (four o'clock) silver knot formation and add two bronze rings.

7 Fold back and angle open the left (eight o'clock) silver knot formation and add two bronze rings. Repeat Steps 1–7, completing a second 18-gauge Tripoli formation.

You can turn the Tripoli into a key fob by adding a split key ring through its two ending rings, as shown.

BEADED (9) TRIPOLI EARRINGS

For the Beaded (9) Tripoli Earrings we assemble the Tripoli formation with 18-gauge tri-metal jump rings and then embellish with them with nine beads—three sets of turquoise and hematite beads, one set on each of the three sides of the Tripoli formation. We use beading cable to thread the beads and secure the cable with a smashed crimp tube. Finally, the beaded Tripolis will be added to earring backs for an eye-catching pair of earrings.

Tools: Two flat-nose pliers, two chain-nose pliers, and side cutters.

Materials: Forty 18-gauge, 3.5mm ID jump rings (four copper, twenty-four silver, twelve bronze); six 6mm turquoise beads; twelve 3mm hematite beads; two 5-inch beading cables; two crimp tubes; and two earring backs.

Note: To make your own headpins, see page 154.

1 Start with two 18-gauge Tripoli formations, each containing twenty 18-gauge, 3.5mm jump rings, two copper, six bronze, and twelve silver rings, following Steps 1–7 of the tri-metal Tripoli formation (see page 63).

2 In this order, add one 3mm hematite bead, one 6mm turquoise bead, and one 3mm hematite bead onto the beading cable, and then run both ends of the cable up through the lower ending bronze rings of the Tripoli formation.

3 In this order, add one 3mm hematite bead, one 6mm turquoise bead, and one 3mm hematite bead onto right side of the beading cable.

4 In this order, add one 3mm hematite bead, one 6mm turquoise bead, and one 3mm hematite bead onto the opposite (left) side of the beading cable. Run the right side of the beading cable through the top ending bronze rings of the Tripoli formation, and then add one crimp tube to the beading cable.

5 Run the left side of the beading cable through the crimp tube, overlapping the right side of the beading cable in a full circle.

6 Run the left side of the beading cable through the top ending bronze rings of the Tripoli formation, then pull both ends of the beading cable to tighten the cable so that the crimp tube is positioned inside the top bronze rings.

7   **Left:** Smash the crimp tube between the top bronze rings to secure the beading cable.

8   **Right:** Continue running both ends of the beading cable in a continuous circle, down through the next 3mm hematite and 6mm turquoise beads. Using side cutters, trim off the excess beading cable just past both 6mm turquoise beads.

9   Add the earring back through the Tripoli's ending bronze pair of rings, as shown. The bead placement limits access to these rings, so the earring back must be added backward. Starting with the small loop opened, run the point of the earring back through the ending pair, then swivel the large loop of the earring back through, finally bringing the small loop of the earring back around the ending pair. Close the small loop with chain-nose pliers.

10   Repeat Steps 1–9 to create a matching pair of earrings.

Here are some alternative gemstone combinations for the 18-gauge silver Tripoli formations (clockwise from top left): 3mm and 6mm blue lapis lazuli beads, 3mm and 6mm red carnelian beads, 3mm clear quartz beads and 6mm amethyst beads, 3mm clear quartz beads and 6mm moss agate beads, 3mm black onyx beads and 6mm red carnelian beads, and 3mm and 6mm black onyx beads.

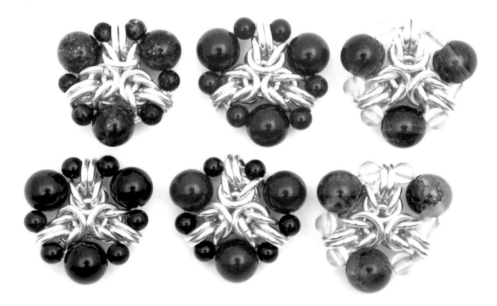

SIMPLE BEADED (3) TRIPOLI FORMATION

A simplified beading technique for the Tripoli formation is to use just three 5mm beads around the formation, rather than the nine used in the Beaded (9) Tripoli Earrings (see page 64). This simplified bead setting allows room to connect one beaded Tripoli form to another through the ending pair of rings, which would not be possible with a beaded (9) placement as we saw when adding the earring back to the Beaded (9) Tripoli Earrings.

Tools: Two flat-nose pliers, chain-nose pliers, and side cutters.

Materials: Twenty 18-gauge, 3.5mm ID bronze jump rings (shown in copper, silver, and bronze in the photos below); three 5mm green jade beads; one 5-inch beading cable; and one crimp tube.

1 Start with an 18-gauge Tripoli formation (see page 63) containing twenty 18-gauge bronze rings (shown here as two copper, twelve silver, and six bronze). Add one 5mm jade bead onto the beading cable and run both ends of the cable up through the bottom end rings of the Tripoli formation, each end traveling through three rings—one silver (angled-open) and the ending bronze pair, at both sides.

2 Run both ends of the beading cable up through the next silver (angled-open) rings so the wire is close against the Tripoli formation and ready to receive the next jade bead.

3 Add the second 5mm jade bead onto the beading cable on the right side of the formation; thread the cable through the next silver (angled-open) ring and the top bronze pair of rings.

4 Add the third 5mm jade bead onto the beading cable on the left side of the formation; add a crimp tube onto the right side of the cable.

5 Run the left side of the beading cable up through the adjacent silver (angled-open) ring and then through the crimp tube, overlapping the right side of the beading cable, being sure to keep the crimp tube between the top bronze pair of rings that terminate the Tripoli formation.

6 Using two chain-nose pliers, one in each hand, grip both ends of the beading cable to pull any slack, until all the beads are tight against the Tripoli formation.

7 **Left:** Smash the crimp tube with the tips of the chain-nose pliers. Continue running both ends of the beading cable through the neighboring jade beads in an overlapping circle. Use the chain-nose pliers to grip the cable and push it through the bead's hole. If the end of the beading cable starts to fray, trim off the fray with side cutters.

8 **Right:** Finally, using side cutters, trim off the excess beading cable just past both 5mm jade beads. The completed Simple Beaded (3) Tripoli formation.

Here are a few alternative gemstone combinations for the Simple Beaded (3) Tripoli formation (clockwise from the top): 5mm green jade, 5mm black onyx, and 5mm faceted garnet beads.

BEADED TRIPOLI BRACELET

The Beaded Tripoli Bracelet combines nine Simple
Beaded (3) Tripoli formations (see page 67) into a
linear chain length, linked by individual large rings.
I illustrate two different approaches to this linear
assembly—*repetitive* (all the Tripolis face the same
direction) and *alternating* (the Tripolis face down,
up, down, up) for a more dynamic aesthetic.

Tools: Two flat-nose pliers, chain-nose pliers, and side
cutters.

Materials: One hundred eighty 18-gauge, 3.5mm ID bronze
jump rings; eleven 14-gauge, 5.5mm ID bronze jump rings;
twenty-seven 5mm green jade beads; nine 5-inch beading
cables; nine crimp tubes; and one bronze S-clasp, to make
a nine-formation, 8-inch bracelet.

1 Start by assembling nine 18-gauge bronze Tripoli formations (see page 63), each set with three 5mm jade beads.

2 Place all nine Tripoli formations in the same direction in a repeating pattern, and connect them using a single 14-gauge brass ring (shown in copper) between each formation. Add S-clasp and catch rings (see page 29) to finish the bracelet. When the beaded Tripoli formations are connected in a straight, repeating pattern, the weight is shifted to the bottom side of the chain, where two beads hang, and the chain might flip and twist on the wrist; possibly better suited for a necklace.

3 For a more organic feel, *alternate* the direction of the nine Tripolis, top bead up, top bead down, etc., and connect them using a single 14-gauge brass ring between each formation. Add an S-clasp and catch rings (see page 29) to finish the bracelet. When the beaded Tripoli formations are connected in an alternating pattern, the weight is balanced top to bottom and the chain will not flip over and twist while on the wrist.

JENS PIND BEADED TRIPOLI BRACELET

The Jens Pind Beaded Tripoli Bracelet combines the previously explored beaded Tripoli with a new chain, the Jens Pind chain, made with three metals. In this beaded Tripoli, we'll use a smaller 19-gauge silver jump ring, which can accommodate a setting of three smaller 4mm beads to each Tripoli. These two beaded Tripoli forms will be combined with two lengths of Jens Pind chain, creating a tension between the two beaded Tripolis for an interacting centerpiece in a dynamic bracelet design.

Tools: Two flat-nose pliers, two chain-nose pliers, side cutters, and a length of scrap wire to hold rings open.

Materials: Forty 19-gauge, 3.1mm ID silver jump rings; seventy-eight 16-gauge, 4mm ID jump rings (twenty-six bronze, twenty-six copper, and twenty-six silver); three 15-gauge, 5mm silver catch rings; three 4mm red carnelian beads; three 4mm purple amethyst beads; two 5-inch beading cables; two crimp tubes; and a silver S-clasp, for an 8-inch bracelet.

1 Start with two 19-gauge silver beaded Tripoli formations (see page 67), one set with three amethyst beads and the second set with three red carnelian beads.

2 To start the chain, add one 16-gauge bronze ring to the amethyst Tripoli. You will use 16-gauge rings for Steps 2–7. Add the second (copper) ring through the first (bronze) ring. Add the third (silver) ring through the first (bronze) and (second) copper rings.

3 Add the fourth (bronze) ring through the second (copper) and third (silver) rings. The scrap wire illustrates where and how the fifth (copper) ring is added into the chain; make sure that the fifth (copper) ring travels through the third (silver) and fourth (bronze) rings.

4 Add the fifth (copper) ring through the third (silver) and fourth (bronze) rings. Add the sixth (silver) ring through the fifth (copper) and fourth (bronze) rings. Add the seventh (bronze) ring through the sixth (silver) and fifth (copper rings), making sure that the seventh (bronze) ring stacks at the same angle as the fourth and first (bronze) rings.

5 Add the eighth (copper) ring through the seventh (bronze) and sixth (silver) rings, making sure that the eighth (copper) ring stacks at the same angle as the fifth and second (copper) rings.

6 Add the ninth (silver) ring through the eighth (copper) and seventh (bronze) rings, making sure that the ninth (silver) ring stacks at the same angle as the sixth and third (silver) rings. Continue this Jens Pind chain (Steps 2–6) until you have a 3-inch chain length. Be very certain that each metal's rings are stacking at the same angle throughout the chain pattern.

7   Repeat Steps 2–7 to build a 3-inch Jens Pind chain pattern out from the carnelian Tripoli formation (created in Step 1).

8   Position the carnelian Tripoli over the amethyst Tripoli. Add two 16-gauge silver rings, as shown, one to each of the Jens Pind chain starting points, so that each 16-gauge silver ring travels through the first (bronze) and second (copper) rings and that each faces toward the other beaded Tripoli.

9   Open the 16-gauge silver ring added to the amethyst Tripoli chain in Step 8, and connect it to the carnelian Tripoli formation, as shown.

10   Open the 16-gauge silver ring added to the carnelian Tripoli chain in Step 8, and connect it to the amethyst Tripoli formation, as shown. There should be a slight tension between the two beaded Tripoli formations as the top beads rub together.

11   Finish each Jens Pind length in a copper and then a bronze ring, so the larger diameter 15-gauge silver ring travels through the last copper and bronze rings in color sequence and holds the silver S-clasp (see page 29).

SUSPENDED TRIPOLI BRACELET

The Suspended Tripoli Bracelet sets beads into the Tripoli formation in a third unique way starting with double-loop-around bead settings, and then building Tripoli formations. These beaded Tripoli formations will then be added individually to a simple 1+2+1 chain so that they are suspended like grapes from a vine.

Tools: Two flat-nose pliers, chain-nose pliers, mandrel-tip pliers (3.1mm) or round-nose pliers (marked at a 3.1mm diameter), side cutters, measuring tape, a length of scrap wire to hold rings open, and a felt-tip pen.

Materials: Two hundred forty-two 19-gauge, 3.1mm ID gold jump rings; twenty-four 15-gauge, 5mm ID silver jump rings; eleven 19-gauge, 1½-inch-long gold headpins; eleven 7mm diameter x 9mm long blue quartz beads; and a gold S-clasp, for an 8-inch bracelet.

1 Set eleven blue quartz beads onto eleven 1½-inch gold headpins with the double-loop-around technique (see page 38). Add four 19-gauge gold rings (shown in silver), assembled 2+2, onto the double loop of a bead setting, creating the bottom knot formation of the Tripoli formation.

2 Fold back and angle open the first knot formation, holding it open with a scrap wire.

3 Add two 19-gauge gold rings (shown in copper) through the knot formation.

4 Add eight 19-gauge gold rings (shown in silver) assembled 2+2 onto the center (copper) pair added in Step 3.

5 Add four 19-gauge gold rings, two through each of the folded-back and angled-open knot formations (shown in silver). Repeat Steps 2–6 ten more times to create eleven beaded Tripoli formations.

6 Starting with a paperclip as a beginning point, assemble all the 15-gauge silver rings with a pair of 19-gauge gold rings between, in a 1+2+1+2+1 repeating pattern.

7 Open the first 15-gauge ring and add the *left* ending ring pair of the first Tripoli formation.

8 **Above Middle:** Open the third 15-gauge ring and add the *right* ending ring pair of the first Tripoli formation, then add the left ending ring pair of the second Tripoli formation to the third 15-gauge ring.

9 **Above Right:** Open the fifth 15-gauge ring and add the right ending ring pair of the second Tripoli, then add the left ending ring pair of the third Tripoli. Continue opening every odd-numbered 15-gauge ring to add the Tripolis, adding all of them to the same side of the 1+2+1+2+1 chain pattern. The addition of the Tripoli forms causes all the even-numbered 15-gauge rings to be pushed up and rest on top of each Tripoli formation, balancing the hanging bead aesthetically. Add the S-clasp and catch rings (see page 29).

NAMASTE TRIPOLI
BRACELET AND EARRINGS

The word *Namaste* is a Sanskrit greeting that translates as "I bow to you—the light within me reflects the light within you." It is a common greeting throughout Nepal and India and from yoga instructors. Just as a Yogi would use the term as a metaphysical reflection, I use it to describe the reflection of beaded Tripoli formations radiating out from both sides of the folded-back chain pattern in this design. The Namaste Tripoli Bracelet and Earrings set the beads with a simple double-loop technique and then assemble the Tripoli formations off the bead settings.

Tools: Two flat-nose pliers, two chain-nose pliers, round-nose pliers (2.5mm), and side cutters.

Materials for bracelet: Four hundred forty-four 20-gauge, 2.75mm ID silver jump rings; twenty-four 16-gauge, 4.5mm ID silver jump rings; three 15-gauge, 5mm ID silver jump rings; twenty-two 20-gauge, 1¼-inch silver headpins; twenty-two 4mm faceted amethyst beads; and a silver S-clasp.

Materials for earrings: Eighty 20-gauge, 2.75mm ID silver jump rings; eight 16-gauge, 4.5mm ID silver jump rings; two 20-gauge, 1¼-inch silver headpins (for bead setting); two 19-gauge, 2-inch silver headpins (for earring backs); and two 4mm faceted amethyst beads.

Note: To make your own headpins, see page 154.

(See bracelet instructions on pages 78 and 79 for details.) To make the Namaste Tripoli Earrings, assemble two beaded Tripolis, two Byzantine chain sections, and two matching earring backs. Add four 16-gauge rings, one from each ending pair of the beaded Tripoli formations, then sixteen 20-gauge rings, four onto each of these added 16-gauge rings. Next, add four more 16-gauge rings, one through each set of four 20-gauge rings, folded over the first 16-gauge rings, so the four 20-gauge rings separate with two rings on both sides of the fold-back. Open the folded-back 16-gauge rings and add on the Byzantine chain section for the top of the earring. Add the earring backs to the center pair within the Byzantine chain section to complete these dramatic earrings.

1   Set all twenty-two 4mm beads onto the 20-gauge headpin wires with the double-loop setting technique (see page 36). From the double loop of each bead setting, build a Tripoli formation using eighteen 20-gauge silver rings (see page 63).

2   Starting with a paperclip as a beginning point, add a 16-gauge silver ring (shown in copper) to the paperclip, then connect two 20-gauge beaded Tripoli formations with a single 16-gauge silver ring (shown in copper) between each formation.

3   Add two 20-gauge silver rings to the beginning 16-gauge ring and four 20-gauge silver rings onto the up side of each subsequent 16-gauge ring (shown in copper). Add a 16-gauge ring (shown in bronze) through each set of the just-added 20-gauge silver rings.

4   Fold each 16-gauge ring (shown in bronze) over the top of each 16-gauge ring (shown in copper), allowing the four 20-gauge silver rings to split equally so there are two 20-gauge rings on each side of the 16-gauge rings.

5   Open the first 16-gauge ring (shown in bronze) and connect it through the paperclip. Take one beaded Tripoli formation and add it to the top of the 16-gauge ring, through the Tripoli's bottom left ring pair, keeping the formation on the upper side of the chain. Close the 16-gauge ring.

6   Open the second 16-gauge ring (shown in bronze) and connect the unattached side of the Tripoli added in Step 5, then add the lower left ring pair of the second Tripoli to this same 16-gauge ring, keeping the formation on the upper side of the chain. Close the 16-gauge ring.

7   Open the third 16-gauge ring (shown in bronze) and connect the opposite side of the second Tripoli, then add the lower left ring pair of the third Tripoli to this same 16-gauge ring, keeping the formation on the upper side of the chain. Close the 16-gauge ring.

An Easy Technique for Adding Folded-Back 16-Gauge Rings

Now that you have the Namaste chain pattern established, here is an easier way of adding each folded-back 16-gauge ring pair down the bracelet length.

8 Starting with the chain pattern you created in Steps 1–7 above, add one 16-gauge silver ring (shown in copper) to the ending right 20-gauge silver ring pair of the lower Tripoli formation, then add four 20-gauge silver rings and the left ring pair of the next lower Tripoli formation to that same 16-gauge ring.

9 Add one 16-gauge silver ring (shown in bronze) through the four 20-gauge silver rings added in Step 8.

10 Fold the upper 16-gauge ring (shown in bronze) over the lower 16-gauge ring (shown in copper), splitting the four 20-gauge rings into two pairs of rings, one pair on each side of the foldover.

11 Open the upper 16-gauge ring (shown in bronze) and add the ending right pair of 20-gauge rings of the upper Tripoli added in Step 7 and then the ending left pair of 20-gauge rings of the next upper Tripoli formation. Keep adding 16-gauge rings and the Tripoli formations, following Steps 8–11, until you have a 7-inch length.

12 With limited space to close the 16-gauge rings, you'll need to use two chain-nose pliers to close them properly. Add catch rings and S-clasp (see page 29) to the finished chain length.

5 | Triangle Formations

In this chapter, we assemble Tripoli formations into a variety of three-sided geometric patterns. First we combine three Tripoli formations into a Triangle pattern with an internal three-ring spiral in the Triple Tripoli Triangle Key Fob. For the Crystal Triangle Earrings we'll set crystals with a unique triple-loop-around bead setting technique that dangles from Tripoli triangles. This crystal-dangling Triangle will be the centerpiece of the Golden Triangle Necklace, assembled between two lengths of Byzantine chain. A more organic Triangle with outside fringe is the focus of the Japanese Rose Necklace. The Double Triangle Bracelet combines two Triangle formations with a single larger ring, finished with a tri-tone Jens Pind chain. Repeating Triangles are taken to the next level in the Wide Triangle Bracelet, which combines twelve silver Triangles with the side-by-side Triple Magnetic clasping system. Finally, the magical Incan Triangle Necklace combines three Tripolis points inward, the gaps between filled with a variety of chains, and embellished with blue lapis beads.

ASSEMBLING THE TRIPLE TRIPOLI TRIANGLE FORMATION

The Triple Tripoli Triangle allows three Tripoli formations to be combined point-to-point into a Triangle formation with an inner spiral of three rings.

Tools: Two flat-nose pliers and chain-nose pliers (optional).

Materials: Seventy-two 18-gauge, 3.5mm ID jump rings (thirty-two bronze and twenty each in copper and silver); and six 14-gauge, 5.5mm ID jump rings (one each in bronze and copper, and four in silver).

1 Assemble three 18-gauge Tripoli formations (see page 63), one each in bronze, copper, and silver. Add three 14-gauge rings (shown in silver) to connect the three Tripolis so they all point upward.

2 Add twelve 18-gauge rings (shown in bronze) in three sets of four rings onto each of the 14-gauge rings so they all hang downward.

3 Open one of the outside 14-gauge rings and connect the silver Tripoli to the bronze Tripoli, keeping all three sets of four bronze rings on the inside of the triangle, while all three Tripolis point outward.

4 Now you'll add a three-ring Flower spiral (see page 28) to the inside of the Triangle. Add the first 14-gauge inner ring (shown in copper) through four 18-gauge bronze rings, two from the left and two from the right, as shown, so the inner (copper) ring lies inside the upper (copper) Tripoli. Add all spiraling rings using the bottomwise technique. As you spiral the rings, check to make sure they are all angled left side high.

5 Add the second 14-gauge inner ring (shown in bronze) through the remaining two 18-gauge bronze rings on the left, then through two 18-gauge bronze rings on the bottom, and then behind and upward through the center of the first inner 14-gauge (copper) ring added in Step 4. Notice how the inner rings are spiraling. The spiraling direction is key for placing the third inner ring, which you'll do in Step 6.

6 To complete the Triple Tripoli Triangle, add the third 14-gauge inner ring (shown in silver) bottomwise through the remaining two 18-gauge bronze rings on the top right, then behind and upward through the centers of both the first (copper) and second (bronze) inner rings, and then through the last two 18-gauge bronze rings on the bottom right, closing the third inner (silver) ring between the 18-gauge pairs, as shown.

You can turn this form into a key fob by adding a split key ring to any of the three outer 14-gauge rings.

Copper and bronze will antique to a much darker hue in short order. For my galleries and gift giving, I make the Triangles using all silver rings to keep the overall bling-bling shine, but I keep the tri-metal inner spiral to emphasize the implied motion created by spiraling rings.

CRYSTAL TRIANGLE EARRINGS

The Crystal Triangle Earrings use the Triple Tripoli Triangle formation but with rings of a slightly smaller gauge. We will add a dangling amethyst crystal from each silver Triple Triangle with the triple-loop-around bead-setting technique.

Tools: Two flat-nose pliers, two chain-nose pliers, and round-nose pliers (2.5mm).

Materials: One hundred forty-one 19-gauge, 3.1mm ID silver jump rings; twelve 15-gauge, 5mm ID silver rings; two 20-gauge, 2¾-inch-long silver headpins for the crystal setting; and two 19-gauge, 2-inch-long silver headpins for earring backs.

Note: To make your own headpins, see page 154.

Find a matching pair of yummy gemstone beads. These amethyst crystals, each about ³/₄-inch long, were drilled to string lengthwise. To set the crystals, use the 20-gauge, 2³/₄-inch-long silver headpins. Ideally, I would use 19-gauge headpins, but the diameter of the drilled hole would only allow a finer, 20-gauge wire.

1 **Left:** Set both amethyst crystals with the triple-loop-around technique (see page 40).

2 **Right:** Assemble three 19-gauge silver Tripolis (see page 63), and then connect them with 15-gauge rings, following Steps 1–6 of the Triple Tripoli Triangle formation. (Use 19-gauge rings when those instructions say to use 18-gauge rings, and use 15-gauge rings when those instructions say to use 14-gauge rings.)

3 Add the crystal setting by removing the two ending 19-gauge rings (shown in copper) from any Tripoli and replace them while traveling through the triple loop of the crystal setting. I added the triple loop versus building it into the Tripoli formation so that the crystals will have more dangling swing.

4 Repeat Steps 1–3 to create a second crystal-set Triangle formation, and add earring backs (see page 34), for a matching pair of earrings.

GOLDEN TRIANGLE NECKLACE

The stunning Golden Triangle Necklace features a Triple Tripoli Triangle design made entirely of gold rings, which is set between two lengths of gold Byzantine chain and embellished with a dazzling long, faceted amethyst bead.

Tools: Two flat-nose pliers, chain-nose pliers, mandrel-tip pliers (3.1mm) or round-nose pliers (marked at a 3.1mm diameter), and side cutters.

Materials: Four hundred eighty-six 19-gauge, 3.1mm ID gold rings; nine 15-gauge, 5mm gold rings; one 19-gauge, 2-inch gold headpin; one very yummy gemstone (I used a ¾-inch-long length faceted amethyst); and one gold S-clasp, for a 16-inch necklace.

1 Using seventy-two 19-gauge rings and six 15-gauge rings, assemble a Triple Tripoli Triangle (see page 82).

2 Assemble two 7-inch lengths of Byzantine chain (see page 44) from two hundred ten 19-gauge rings. Set the gemstone with a double-loop-around technique (page 38) and forge a gold S-clasp (see page 29).

3 **Left:** Line up the upper-right Tripoli in the Triangle formation with one end of one 7-inch Byzantine chain length.

4 **Right:** Remove the two pairs of terminating 19-gauge rings from both the upper-right Tripoli and the Byzantine chain.

5 **Left:** Add two 19-gauge rings (shown in copper) connecting the upper-right Tripoli and Byzantine chain length (see page 49).

6 **Right:** Repeat Steps 3–5 to connect the upper-left Tripoli and second length of Byzantine chain.

7 Line up the bottom Tripoli with the double loop of the crystal setting. Remove six 19-gauge rings from the Tripoli, disassembling the lower knot formation at the bottom. Add two of these rings (shown in silver) to the double loop of the crystal setting.

8 (Steps 8, 9, and 10 are one continuous process, broken into three parts.) Using the bottomwise technique (see page 28), add the third 19-gauge ring (shown in copper), hooking the ring behind and up through the lower 19-gauge ring (shown in silver).

9 Continue the same ring through the bottom two 19-gauge rings of the disassembled Tripoli.

10 Continue the same ring through the upper 19-gauge ring (shown in silver) previously added to the double loop of the bead setting. Close this third 19-gauge ring, after it travels through four rings, to serve as one of the folded-back rings of the knot formation.

11 Add the fourth 19-gauge ring (shown in copper) the same way you added the third ring in Steps 8–10, but on the other side of the crystal's double loop, as shown.

12 Try on the necklace so the gold triangle and amethyst hang where desired and lengthen both Byzantine chain lengths as needed. (For each extra inch of Byzantine chain, you will need thirty 19-gauge, 3.1mm gold jump rings). Finally, add the golden S-clasp and catch rings (see page 29).

JAPANESE ROSE NECKLACE

The Japanese Rose Triangle Necklace turns the geometric Triple Tripoli Triangle formation a bit more organic with the addition of fringe rings that round out the Triangle form and allow the addition of individual Japanese Rose forms into the necklace length. We also add an optional gemstone embellishment to the center triangle form.

Tools: Two flat-nose pliers, two chain-nose pliers, mandrel-tip pliers (3.1mm) or round-nose pliers (marked at a 3.1mm diameter), and side cutters.

Materials: Three hundred ninety 19-gauge, 3.1mm ID bronze jump rings; one hundred five 15-gauge, 5mm ID silver jump rings; one 19-gauge, 4¼-inch-long bronze wire to set gemstone (optional); one ¾-inch-wide × 1-inch-tall blue chalcedony gemstone (or large gemstone of your choice) with ½-inch-width drilled hole (optional); and one silver S-clasp, for a 15-inch necklace.

1 Assemble a Triple Tripoli Triangle formation (see page 82) with seventy-two 19-gauge bronze and six 15-gauge silver rings. Add eighteen 19-gauge bronze rings (shown in copper) in three sets of six rings onto each outer 15-gauge silver ring.

2 Add nine 15-gauge silver rings (shown in copper), each one through two of the 19-gauge rings added in Step 1, so there are three 15-gauge rings on each side of the Triangle formation.

3 Add twelve 19-gauge bronze rings (shown in copper), two connecting each of the 15-gauge rings added in Step 2, to complete the Rounded Triangle formation.

4 Assemble a 1+2+1 chain length with six 15-gauge silver rings connected by five pairs of 19-gauge bronze rings between each.

5 Add ten 19-gauge rings (shown in copper) two each added onto five of the six 15-gauge rings, so all added rings are on the bottom side of the 1+2+1 chain length.

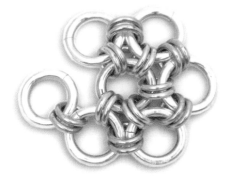

6 Add one 15-gauge ring (shown in copper) through all ten 19-gauge rings added in Step 5.

7 Add four 19-gauge rings (shown in copper)—two rings connect the center 15-gauge ring to the sixth 15-gauge outside ring, and the other two rings connect the sixth outside 15-gauge ring to the first 15-gauge outside ring. This completes one Japanese Rose formation. Repeat Steps 4–7 eleven more times to create twelve Japanese Roses.

8 To add a Japanese Rose, open one 15-gauge outer ring (shown in copper) and hook it through the middle 15-gauge outer ring on one side of the Rounded Triangle form (made in Steps 1–3).

9 Too add the next Japanese Rose, open one 15-gauge outer ring (shown in copper) and hook it through a 15-gauge outer ring of the Rose added in Step 8. Continue connecting the Roses in a sequential chain pattern, six Roses on each side of the Rounded Triangle form. Try on the necklace and lengthen both chain lengths as needed for desired length. Add the catch rings and silver S-clasp (see page 29).

Gemstone Setting for the Necklace (optional)

This gemstone is a blue chalcedony, a gift from "Africa John." Thanks, John.

1 Cut a 4¼-inch length of 19-gauge bronze wire. Mark ½ inch from each end. Using the 3.1mm jaw of the mandrel-tip pliers, grip the wire at the ½-inch mark and bend a double loop-around (see page 38).

2 Measure ³⁄₈ inch from the bottom of the double loop-around and mark. Grip the wire just before the mark and bend it at a 90-degree angle. Note: ³⁄₈ inch is the distance from the drilled hold to the top of the bead.

3 Slide the gemstone onto the wire all the way to the 90-degree bend, and mark the wire at the stone's drilled hole on the opposite side from the bend. Remove the stone.

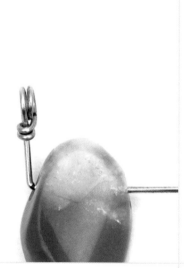

4 Using flat-nose pliers, grip the wire just past the mark made in Step 3 and bend it up at a 90-degree angle.

5 Bend both ends of the wire down to straighten out the wire slightly, just enough to thread it through the gemstone's drilled hole.

6 With the bead on the wire, re-bend the wire upward with your fingers. The 90-degree angles should be precise, as metal wire has a crazy memory for things like that. On the non-double-looped side of the wire, measure up 1³⁄₈ inch and mark; there should be ½ inch of wire beyond the mark.

7 Using the 3.1mm jaw of the mandrel-tip pliers, grip the wire at the mark and bend a double loop in an opposite spiral to the double loop created in Step 2 above, bringing this second double loop even with the first double loop so the bead will hang level. **Note:** The ½-inch tail is on the inside.

8 Wrap the ½-inch tail one and a half times around the base 19-gauge wire in a double-loop-around technique (see page 38).

9 Remove one 15-gauge ring from the bottom of the Rounded Triangle formation, allowing more room. Open the middle 15-gauge ring (shown in copper), remove the two loose 19-gauge rings, and add both double loops of the gemstone setting.

10 Add back the 15-gauge ring (shown in copper) and the two 19-gauge rings (shown in copper) that were removed in Step 9.

DOUBLE TRIANGLE BRACELET

The Double Triangle Bracelet combines two Triple Tripoli Triangle formations into a Double Triangle formation with the addition of a single larger diameter ring between the two Triangles. The first Triangle is assembled with copper rings, and the second Triangle is assembled with silver rings to emphasize a duality, which is set off with a tri-metal Jens Pind chain connected to the Double Triangle formation with a golden magnetic clasp.

Tools: Two flat-nose pliers.

Materials: One hundred forty-four 19-gauge, 3.1mm ID jump rings (seventy-two copper, seventy-two silver); twelve 15-gauge, 5mm ID jump rings (six each in copper and silver); sixty 16-gauge, 4mm ID jump rings (twenty each in copper, silver, and bronze); one 15-gauge, 5.5mm ID bronze center ring; and a golden magnetic clasp, for an 8-inch bracelet.

1 Using seventy-two 19-gauge and six 15-gauge copper rings, assemble one copper Triple Tripoli Triangle formation (see page 82) and, using sixty 19-gauge silver rings, assemble three silver Tripoli formations (see page 63).

2 Replace one of the outside 15-gauge, 5mm copper rings in the Triangle with a 15-gauge, 5.5mm bronze ring. This larger ring will allow the next (silver) Triangle to be assembled.

3 Onto this 15-gauge bronze ring, add on the first and second silver Tripoli forms of the Triangle. Add four 19-gauge silver rings onto this same 15-gauge bronze ring, between the two silver Tripolis.

4 Add one 15-gauge silver ring to connect the outside of the second Tripoli to the third Tripoli, then add four 19-gauge silver rings to that 15-gauge ring between the second and third Tripolis, keeping the Tripoli's pointed outward and the added 19-gauge rings on the inside of the Triangle, as shown.

5 Add one 15-gauge silver ring to connect the third Tripoli back to the first Tripoli, and add four 19-gauge silver rings between the two Tripolis, keeping all three sets of four 19-gauge rings pointing inward, while all three Tripolis point outward into a Triangle shape.

6 To form the inner three-ring Flower Spiral (see page 28), add three 15-gauge silver rings to the center of the Triangle. Add all spiraling rings using the bottomwise technique. As you spiral the rings, check to make sure they are all angled left side high.

7 Add two 16-gauge bronze rings, one on each side, to connect the unconnected points of the copper and silver triangles.

8 Starting at the outside point of the silver Triangle and using 16-gauge copper, bronze, and silver rings, assemble the Jens Pind chain pattern (see page 72 or 156), keeping the metal sequence of copper, bronze, silver.

9 Continue the Jens Pind chain, keeping each metal in a consistent stacking pattern, until the chain is 7 inches long.

10 Add the gold magnetic clasp (see page 38) to the chain and, with one 16-gauge silver ring, to the copper Triangle to complete the bracelet.

WIDE TRIANGLE BRACELET WITH TRIPLE MAGNETIC CLASP

The Wide Triangle Bracelet continues the concept of repeating Triangle formations but uses finer gauges of silver rings and alternates the orientation of each of the twelve Triangles to create a seamless 1-inch-wide bracelet. This bracelet terminates in a unique Triple Magnetic Clasp, which features three magnetic tubes at one end of the bracelet that connect side by side with three magnetic tubes of opposite polarity at the other end.

Tools: Two flat-nose pliers, two chain-nose pliers, round-nose pliers (marked at 2.5mm diameter), side cutters, a felt-tip pen, and measuring tape.

Materials: Eight hundred sixty-four 20-gauge, 2.75mm ID silver jump rings; sixty-four 16-gauge, 4.5mm ID silver jump rings; and eleven 16-gauge, 5.25mm ID silver jump rings, for an 8-inch bracelet.

Tools for magnetic clasp: Round-nose pliers (marked at 2.5mm), chain-nose pliers, side cutters, measuring tape, and a felt-tip marker.

Materials for magnetic clasp: Two 20-gauge, 3¼-inch-long silver wire lengths and six 6mm silver magnetic beads.

1 Assemble thirty-six Tripolis, each containing twenty 20-gauge silver rings. Create the first Triple Tripoli Triangle (see page 82, Steps 1–6) with twelve 20-gauge rings and six 16-gauge rings. Two 16-gauge, 4.5mm rings connect the Tripolis on the left and bottom, and one 16-gauge, 5.25mm ring (shown in bronze) connects the Tripolis on the right, as shown. Three 16-gauge, 4.5mm rings form the center three-ring spiraling Flower formation (see page 28). Add all spiraling rings using the bottomwise technique. As you spiral the rings, check to make sure they are all angled left side high.

2 Open the 16-gauge, 5.25mm bronze ring added to the first Triangle form in Step 1 and add two of the three Tripolis from the second Triangle to it. Add the third Tripoli of the second Triangle with one 16-gauge, 4.5mm ring and one 16-gauge, 5.25mm ring (shown in bronze on the right). Complete the second Triangle and center spiraling rings as you completed the first Triangle (see Step 1).

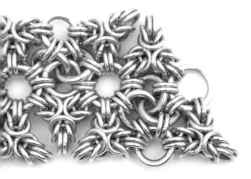

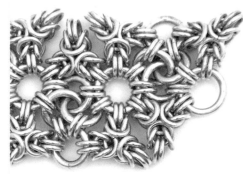

3 Assemble the third Triangle and spiraling center rings exactly as you did the first and second Triangles (in Steps 1 and 2), adding a 16-gauge, 5.25mm ring (shown in bronze on the right), ready for the fourth Triangle.

4 Following Steps 1–3 above, add the fourth Triangle and assemble its center spiraling rings. Continue the pattern by adding Triangles in this manner until you assemble all twelve Triangles.

5 Add 16-gauge, 4.5mm rings (shown in copper) to connect each of the outside tips of the Triangles.

6 You need an even number of Triangles so the open ends of the chain meet at a 45-degree angle for the clasping system.

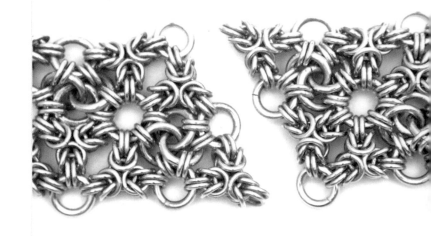

Triple Magnetic Clasping System

7 Cut the 20-gauge silver wire into two 3¼-inch lengths. Use a felt-tip marker to mark each wire ¼ inch from each end. Using the round-nose pliers at 2.5mm diameter, grip a 20-gauge wire at the first ¼-inch mark and bend a double-loop-around wire technique around the jaw (see page 38). Bend the double loop at a 30-degree angle from the remaining wire length.

8 Add the three magnetic beads onto the 20-gauge wire, measure ⅞ inch beyond the beads, and mark the wire with the felt-tip pen; you should have ¼ inch of wire beyond this mark.

9 Using the round-nose pliers at a 2.5mm diameter, grip the 20-gauge wire at the mark made in Step 8 and bend a double loop around the jaw (see page 36), till the double loop is almost touching the magnetic beads; wrap the remaining ¼-inch tail between the beads and double loop, and trim the end of the wire.

10 Bend this second double loop at a 30-degree angle from the beads, angling the same direction as the first double loop. Repeat Steps 7–10 to create a second wire setting of three magnetic beads. This second set should have opposite magnetic polarity so they are attracted side by side.

11 Using 16-gauge, 4.5mm silver rings, add the magnetic clasping system to the ends of the Wide Triangle Bracelet.

INCAN TRIANGLE NECKLACE

The Incan Triangle Necklace is the actualization of my pursuit of the mystery of what is possible. My goal was to figure out a way to combine three Tripoli formations pointing *inward* and then artfully fill the huge gaps that result from that placement. In this design, those gaps are filled with three overlapping rings extending from Triangle point to Triangle point; the resulting three internal negative spaces, and the three sides of the Incan Triangle, are then filled by six groups of lapis lazuli beads, for a truly one-of-a-kind beaded Triangle formation. The Incan Triangle is finished with two lengths of Inca Puño chain, terminated with an S-clasp.

Tools: Two flat-nose pliers, two chain-nose pliers, and side cutters.

Materials: Eighty-four 18-gauge, 3.5mm ID bronze jump rings (for the Tripoli formations); six 16-gauge, 4.5mm ID bronze jump rings; nine 14-gauge, 5.5mm ID bronze jump rings (for the Inca Puño chain); three hundred sixty-eight 18-gauge, 4.5mm bronze rings (for the Inca Puño chain); three 15-gauge, 5mm bronze catch rings; six round 6mm lapis lazuli beads; twelve round 3mm lapis lazuli beads; one 7-inch beading cable; one crimp tube; and one bronze S-clasp, for a 16-inch necklace.

1 Assemble three Tripoli formations, each consisting of twenty 18-gauge, 3.5mm bronze jump rings. Add two 18-gauge, 3.5mm rings (shown in copper) in an interlocking spiral, to connect the first and second Tripoli forms.

2 Add a third 18-gauge, 3.5mm ring (shown in copper) to connect the third Tripoli form, spiraling from behind and up through the previous two 18-gauge rings in a consistent left-side high Flower spiral (see page 28), as you look from each Tripoli inward.

3 Add one 14-gauge, 5.5mm ring with four 18-gauge, 3.5mm rings (all shown in copper) onto each of the three Tripoli forms, as shown. Looking from the outside inward, add them onto the right side of each Tripoli, without un-spiraling the inner Flower formation.

4 Add a second 14-gauge, 5.5mm (shown in copper) through the four 18-gauge (bronze) rings added in Step 3. Flip this second 14-gauge ring over and on top of the first 14-gauge (bronze) ring, splitting the four 18-gauge rings added in Step 3 into two pairs, one pair on each side of the overlap. To keep this overlap from unfolding, add four new 18-gauge, 3.5mm rings (shown in copper) to the second 14-gauge ring added in this step.

5 To close up the exterior Triangle shape, add a third 14-gauge, 5.5mm ring (shown in copper) through each of the four 18-gauge rings added in Step 4. Flip this third 14-gauge ring over and on top of the second 14-gauge ring (added in Step 4), splitting the four 18-gauge rings added in Step 4 into two pairs, one pair on each side of the overlap. Next, open this third 14-gauge ring and attach it the next Tripoli, as shown, without un-spiraling the inner Flower formation.

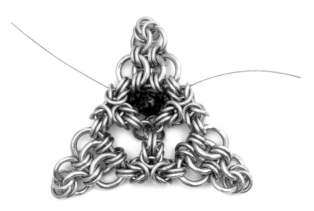

6 Add two 16-gauge, 4.5mm rings (shown in copper), each through the two outermost 18-gauge rings of the chain pattern connecting the Tripolis, as shown. Next, add two or three 18-gauge, 3.5mm rings (shown in copper) through the two 16-gauge rings to terminate each of the three points of the Triangle formation.

7 In this order, add one 3mm, one 6mm, and one 3mm lapis lazuli bead to the beading cable, and then run both ends of the cable from the inside outward through four rings of the upper Tripoli forms (similarly to Step 2 of the Simple Beaded [3] Tripoli, page 67).

8 In this order, add one 3mm, one 6mm, and one 3mm lapis lazuli bead onto the right side and then onto the left side of the beading cable.

9 On both the right and left sides of the Triangle formation, run the beading cable from the outside inward through the two knot formations of the upper Tripoli forms into the two lower open spaces.

10 In this order, add one 3mm, one 6mm, and one 3mm lapis lazuli bead, onto both the right and the left side of the beading cable and then run the cable outside the Triangle through the knots of the lower Tripoli formation, as shown.

11 Pull the left cable out of the 18-gauge ring at the bottom of the lower knot, then add on a crimp tube and loop the cable back through the original 18-gauge ring, as shown. (The crimp tube will be hidden inside the Tripoli, so the beads can lay tight against the metal pattern.) Add the last (bottom) set of one 3mm, one 6mm, and one 3mm lapis lazuli beads onto the right cable.

12 Run the right side of the beading cable through the lower-left 18-gauge ring of the Tripoli and then through the crimp tube you added in Step 11, in an overlapping circle. Pull the beading cable taut so all the six bead sets are tight against the metal pattern.

13 Smash the crimp tube with the tips of chain-nose pliers. Run both cable ends through the neighboring beads in an overlapping circle, and then carefully trim off the excess cable with the side cutters.

14 The finished beaded Incan Triangle is indeed an epic pattern, especially in this bronze and lapis combination. Now you are ready to add the Inca Puño chains.

15 Using one hundred eighty-four 18-gauge, 4.5mm bronze rings, assemble two 7-inch Inca Puño chain lengths (see page 157). Add the chain lengths to the necklace centerpiece through their two terminating 18-gauge rings added in Step 6. Add a bronze S-clasp and catch rings (see page 29) to the opposite ends of the chain lengths to finish the necklace.

6 Quatrefoil and Trapezoid Formations

In this chapter, we assemble Tripoli formations into a variety of four-sided geometric patterns. The basic Beaded Quatrefoil formation comprises four bronze Tripoli forms with four rings spiraling in the center and is set with amethyst beads. The Quatrefoil Bracelet combines four beaded Quatrefoil formations with smaller spirals between them in a linear bracelet length, while the Flower Quatrefoil Earrings combine four Tripolis with four Small Flower formations around a single large central Flower formation. Next, we unfold a Flower Quatrefoil into what I call the Ocean Bracelet, starting with four Tripolis connected by five Small Flower formations attached to a wave pattern of five Large Flower formations. Each cresting wave is then set with a variety of green aventurine beads and a Venetian glass bead for visual buoyancy. The final two projects combine three Tripoli formations and two Byzantine chain sections into a Trapezoid formation. This formation is set with turquoise beads in the Trapezoid Beaded Key Fob, and a repeating pattern of the formation is set with garnet beads in the Trapezoid Beaded Bracelet.

ASSEMBLING THE BEADED QUATREFOIL FORMATION

The Quatrefoil formation combines four bronze Tripoli forms so they all point outward to create a hollow square in the center that is filled with a four-ring spiral. The gap between this inner spiral and each of the Tripolis is the perfect size for a 6mm bead.

Tools: Two flat-nose pliers, two chain-nose pliers, and side cutters.

Materials: Eighty-eight 18-gauge, 3.5m ID bronze jump rings; eight 14-gauge, 5.5mm ID bronze jump rings; four 6mm faceted black onyx beads; one 5-inch beading cable; and one crimp tube.

1 **Left:** ssemble four Tripoli formations (see page 63), each consisting of twenty 18-gauge rings. Combine the four Tripolis, as shown, with four 14-gauge rings (shown in copper), so all four Tripolis are pointing outward in a Quatrefoil shape.

2 **Right:** Add eight 18-gauge rings (shown in copper), two rings onto the inside of each 14-gauge ring. These ring pairs are identified, in counterclockwise order, for techniques in Steps 3–13: *top*, *left*, *bottom*, and *right*.

3 To begin the inner four-ring Flower spiral (see page 28), add one 14-gauge ring (shown in copper) through the *top* pair of 18-gauge rings as the first inner-spiral ring. Add all spiraling rings using the bottomwise technique. As you spiral the rings, check to make sure they are all angled left side high (see page 28).

4 Add a second 14-gauge ring (shown in copper) to the center spiral through the *left* pair of 18-gauge rings and up through the center of the first 14-gauge ring added in Step 3.

5 **Left:** Add the third 14-gauge ring (shown in copper) through the *bottom* pair of 18-gauge rings and up through the center of the first and second 14-gauge rings (added in Steps 3 and 4).

6 **Right:** Add the fourth 14-gauge ring (shown in copper) through the *right* pair of 18-gauge rings and up through the center of the first, second, and third 14-gauge rings (added in Steps 3, 4, and 5).

Beading the Quatrefoil

7 You will saddle beads between the four Tripolis, tightening or loosing the inner four-ring spiral depending on bead sizing. We'll use 6mm beads. Add the first 6mm faceted black onyx bead into the upper right space by running the beading cable through the *top* and *right* pairs of 18-gauge rings (added in step 2).

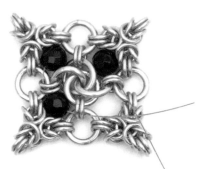

8 **Left:** Add the second bead to the left end of the cable and run it into the upper left space of the Quatrefoil, then thread the beading cable through the *left* pair of 18-gauge rings.

9 **Right:** Add the third bead to the left end of the cable and run it into the lower left space of the Quatrefoil, then thread the beading cable through the *bottom* pair of 18-gauge rings.

10 Add the fourth bead to the left end of the cable followed by a crimp tube, as shown.

11 Bring the right (opposite) end of the beading cable through the crimp tube and then through the fourth bead in an overlapping circle, as shown.

12 **Left:** Pull the cable from both ends so all four beads are snug within the Quatrefoil. Take care to not overtighten this bead setting, allowing all four beads to lay flat without restricting the chain formation.

13 **Right:** Position the crimp tube between the *right* pair of 18-gauge rings, and smash the tube with the short chain-nose pliers tips, as shown. Using side cutters, trim off the excess beading cable just past the neighboring beads.

BEADED QUATREFOIL BRACELET

The Quatrefoil Bracelet combines four finer-gauge silver Quatrefoil formations connected side by side with larger bronze rings and is set with 6mm faceted amethyst beads. After the bracelet project, we'll discuss an alternative way the Quatrefoils could be connected into a bracelet length.

Tools: Two flat-nose pliers, two chain-nose pliers, and side cutters.

Materials for bracelet (four formations): Three hundred eighty-eight 19-gauge, 3.1mm ID silver jump rings; forty-seven 15-gauge, 5mm ID bronze jump rings; eighteen 16-gauge, 4.5mm ID silver jump rings; sixteen 6mm faceted amethyst beads; four 5-inch beading cables; four crimp tubes; and a bronze S-clasp.

Materials for bracelet assembled in diamond pattern (six formations): Five hundred twenty-eight 19-gauge, 3.1mm ID silver jump rings; fifty 15-gauge, 5mm ID bronze jump rings; twenty-four 6mm faceted amethyst beads; six 5-inch beading cables; six crimp tubes; and a bronze S-clasp.

1 Following Steps 1–13 of the Quatrefoil formation (see page 106), make four beaded Quatrefoil formations. When those instructions call for 18-gauge rings, you'll use 19-gauge silver rings instead. When those instructions call for 14-gauge rings, you'll use 15-gauge bronze rings instead. Lay the first Quatrefoil on your work surface, oriented on its side to look like a square, as shown.

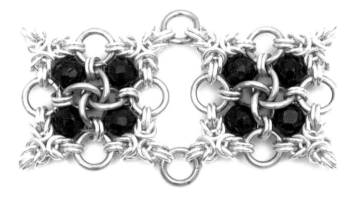

2 Connect the second Quatrefoil to the first, side by side, with two 15-gauge rings (shown in copper), one each at the top and bottom adjacent corners. Connect the remaining two Quatrefoils in the same manner until you have a 7-inch length.

3 Add eight 19-gauge rings (shown in copper), two onto the inside of each of the four 15-gauge rings, and then spiral four 16-gauge rings (shown in copper) from the eight 19-gauge rings, as shown. Continue in this manner along the entire 7-inch length. Add all spiraling rings using the bottomwise technique (see page 28). As you spiral the rings, check to make sure they are all angled left side high.

4 Terminate one end of the bracelet design by adding three pair of 19-gauge rings and a four-ring spiral of 16-gauge rings. Connect the small loop of the bronze S-clasp (see page 29) to the fourth ring of the ending small spiral. Terminate the opposite end of the bracelet by adding three pairs of 19-gauge rings and a four-ring spiral of 16-gauge rings, adding two 15-gauge catch rings (assembled 1+1) onto the fourth 16-gauge ring.

Diamond Orientation Assembly Variation

Note: With this assembly method, you'll need six (not four) Quatrefoil forms for a 7-inch bracelet length.

1 This overlapping Quatrefoil design connects the Quatrefoils in a diamond orientation, rather than a square orientation. Open a 15-gauge ring on the first Quatrefoil and add the 19-gauge ring pair at the point of the second Quatrefoil, as shown.

2 Open the adjacent 15-gauge ring (shown in copper) on the second Quatrefoil and add the 19-gauge ring pair at the point of the first Quatrefoil, as shown.

3 Continue to assemble Quatrefoils in this manner until you have a 7-inch bracelet length. Add the S-clasp and catch rings (see page 29).

FLOWER QUATREFOIL EARRINGS

The Flower Quatrefoil Earrings combine gold rings with complementary lapis lazuli beads. Four Tripolis joined with four 19-gauge Small Flower formations to form the frame of the Quatrefoil, with a 17-gauge Large Flower formation added in the center. We will set a 10mm lapis lazuli bead from each Flower Quatrefoil and finish the earrings with gold earring backs.

Tools: Two flat-nose pliers, two chain-nose pliers, and mandrel-tip pliers (3.1mm).

Materials: One hundred sixty 19-gauge, 3.1mm ID gold jump rings (for the Tripolis); forty-eight 19-gauge, 3.9mm ID gold jump rings (for the Small Flower forms); six 17-gauge, 8.75mm ID gold jump rings (for the Large Flower forms); four 19-gauge, 2-inch-long gold headpins (two for bead setting and two for earring backs); and two 10mm lapis lazuli beads.

1 Assemble four Tripolis (see page 63), each consisting of twenty 19-gauge, 3.1mm gold rings. In Steps 1–3, you will connect the Tripolis with spiraling three-ring Small Flower forms (see page 28). Connect two Tripolis with a single 19-gauge, 3.9mm ring (shown in copper).

2 Add a second 19-gauge, 3.9mm ring (shown in copper) to connect both Tripolis, spiralling around the first ring. Add all spiraling rings using the bottomwise technique (see page 28). As you spiral the rings, check to make sure they are all angled left side high.

3 Add a third 19-gauge ring the same way you added the second ring. Close the third ring flush for a three-ring spiraling Small Flower.

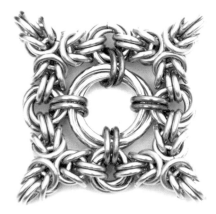

4 **Left:** Repeat Steps 1–3 to connect all four Tripolis with four Small Flowers.

5 **Right:** Add eight 19-gauge, 3.9mm rings (shown in copper), two rings to the inside of each Small Flower formation, to connect a Large Flower formation (see page 28) of three spiraling 17-gauge rings to the center of the Quatrefoil, as shown.

6 **Left:** Add four 19-gauge, 3.9mm rings (shown in copper), one ring to each corner of the Tripoli. These rings will keep the sides from drooping down when the Flower Quatrefoils are worn as earrings.

7 **Right:** Add the small loop of the earring back (see page 34) to the top Tripoli to finish the earring. Add an optional double loop bead setting (see page 38) to the bottom rings. Repeat Steps 1–7 to create a matching pair of earrings.

OCEAN BRACELET

The Ocean Bracelet unravels the Flower Quatrefoil formation into three Wave formations that will be set with a variety of beads. Similar to the Flower Quatrefoil, each Wave will start with four Tripolis, connected by Small Flower formations and attached to five Large Flower formations, but instead of forming a square shape, we'll form a cresting wave shape. Each of these three cresting Wave formations is then set with a variety of green aventurine and one Venetian Glass bead for visual buoyancy.

Tools: Two flat-nose pliers, two chain-nose pliers, and side cutters.

Materials: Two hundred forty 19-gauge, 3.1mm ID silver jump rings (for twelve Tripolis); forty-five 19-gauge, 3.9mm ID gold jump rings (for fifteen Small Flowers); sixty-one 17-gauge, 8.75mm ID bronze jump rings (for seventeen Large Flowers); forty-seven 17-gauge, 4mm ID silver jump rings (to connect Large Flowers); three 15-gauge, 5mm ID bronze catch rings; nine 4mm faceted green aventurine; nine 6mm diameter × 4mm wide green aventurine; nine 4mm wide × 16mm long green aventurine; three 9mm Venetian glass beads (clear with blue swirl); three 9-inch beading cables; six crimp tubes; and one bronze S-clasp, for an 8-inch bracelet.

1 Following Steps 1–4 of the Flower Quatrefoil Earrings (see page 112), create four Tripolis from 19-gauge, 3.1mm silver jump rings. Connect each of the four Tripolis with a three-ring spiraling Small Flower (see page 28) from 19-gauge, 3.9mm gold jump rings, adding a fifth Small Flower on the ending Tripoli in a linear chain, as shown. Add all spiraling rings using the bottomwise technique. As you spiral the rings, check to make sure they are all angled left side high.

2 You'll create the first two Large Flowers of the chain in Steps 2–4. Connect two individual 17-gauge, 8.75mm bronze rings (shown in copper) with one 17-gauge, 4mm silver ring.

3 Add a second 17-gauge, 8.75mm bronze ring (shown in silver) to each of the 17-gauge rings added in Step 2, spiraling in bottomwise technique.

4 Add a third 17-gauge, 8.75mm bronze ring to the first two added in Steps 2 and 3, spiraling in bottomwise technique.

5 Continue this Large Flower chain pattern into a five-Flower chain length. Connect the last (fifth) Large Flower back to the third Large Flower with a 17-gauge, 4mm silver ring, as shown.

6 Assemble the gold Small Flowers to the bronze Large Flowers with two 17-gauge, 4mm silver rings added to each Small Flower; connect one ring to the first Large Flower and the other to the second Large Flower, as shown, snuggling the Small Flower between two Large Flowers. Continue until all are assembled, creating a Wave formation. Repeat Steps 1–6 twice to make three Waves.

Beading the Ocean Bracelet

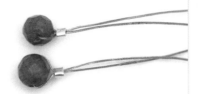

7 To each of the three Wave formations created in Steps 1–6 above, in this order, add one 4mm faceted green aventurine bead and one crimp bead onto a 9-inch beading cable. Run the cable in a loop around the bead and back through the crimp tube, as shown. Adjust the cable so one end is only an inch long and bring the crimp tube tight against the bead before you smash it in place, creating a plug bead.

8 Run both lengths of beading cable through the first Tripoli till the plug bead is tight against the Tripoli. On the other side of the Tripoli, add one 4mm x 6mm green aventurine disk bead to both wire lengths and then trim the shorter end just past this second bead. Run the beading cable through the second Tripoli form.

9 Add one 4mm x 6mm green aventurine disk bead and then one 9mm Venetian glass bead to the beading cable, and run the cable though the third Tripoli form.

10 In this order, add one 4mm faceted green aventurine bead, one 16mm x 4mm oval green aventurine bead, one 4mm x 6mm green aventurine disk bead, and two 16mm x 4mm oval green aventurine beads (for a total of 20mm of bead length).

11 Run the beading cable through the ending pair of rings of the fourth Tripoli, and add a crimp tube and then a 4mm faceted green aventurine bead.

12 Run the beading cable around the 4mm faceted bead and back through the crimp tube, then back through the silver ring pair of the Tripoli and back through two 16mm aventurine oval beads.

13 Carefully tighten the beading cable until you can smash the crimp tube (with the tip of the chain-nose pliers) between the silver rings, as shown, and trim off excess cable past the two aventurine oval beads with side cutters. Add catch rings and the S-clasp (see page 29) to finish.

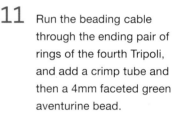

TRAPEZOID KEY FOB

The Trapezoid Key Fob will be assembled with three Tripoli forms and two Byzantine chain sections into a four-sided form. This form is then set with five blue turquoise beads: four 4mm on the inside and the fifth 6mm turquoise bead on the top.

Tools: Two flat-nose pliers, two chain-nose pliers, and side cutters.

Materials: Eighty-eight 19-gauge, 3.1mm ID bronze rings; nine 16-gauge, 4mm ID bronze rings; one 14-gauge, 5.5mm bronze ring; one split key ring; one 6mm turquoise and four 4mm beads; one crimp tube; and one 5-inch beading cable.

1 Assemble three 19-gauge bronze Tripoli formations (see page 63), each consisting of twenty 19-gauge rings. Assemble two 19-gauge bronze Byzantine formations (see page 44), each consisting of fourteen 19-gauge rings. Combine three Tripolis and one Byzantine chain section with one 16-gauge bronze ring (shown in copper).

2 **Above left:** Assemble the second bronze Byzantine chain length to the center 16-gauge bronze ring by disassembling and then reassembling the two ending pairs of 19-gauge rings (shown in copper).

3 **Above Right:** Add eight 16-gauge bronze rings (shown in copper), two rings at each of the four outside points of the formation, as shown.

Beading the Trapezoid

4 **Left:** Start the bead embellishment by running the beading cable through the upper-left Byzantine, then add a single 4mm bead and run the cable through the adjoining Tripoli.

5 **Right:** Add the second 4mm bead and then run the beading cable through the bottom Tripoli.

6 Add the third 4mm bead and then the fourth 4mm bead in the same manner and continue running the beading cable up through the upper-right Byzantine chain.

7 Add the 6mm bead and a crimp tube to one end of the beading cable.

8 **Left:** Run the opposite end of the beading cable through the crimp tube in an overlapping circle, as shown.

9 **Right:** Run the cable ends through the two adjacent beads, pull both cables taut, and smash the crimp tube with the chain-nose pliers; trim off the excess beading cable with side cutters. Add the split key ring with the 14-gauge bronze ring for a finished key fob.

TRAPEZOID BRACELET

The Trapezoid Bracelet combines the four-sided
formation in a repeating chain pattern to form
a 1-inch-wide bracelet, setting each form in an
alternating pattern down the chain length. This
alternating placement allows the wide bracelet
length to lay straight instead of curving like the
Pentagon Necklace on page 126. Each Trapezoid
form is set with five red garnet beads, four 3.3mm
beads within the form, and a fifth larger 5mm
faceted garnet bead on the outside between the two
Byzantine chain sections.

Tools: Flat-nose pliers, two chain-nose pliers,
and side cutters.

Materials: Six hundred sixteen 20-gauge, 2.75mm
ID silver jump rings; twenty-four 16-gauge, 3.5mm ID
bronze rings; three 14-gauge, 5.5mm ID silver jump
rings; twenty-eight 3.3mm round garnet beads; seven
5mm round, faceted garnet beads; seven 5-inch beading
cables; five crimp tubes; and one silver S-clasp, for an
8-inch bracelet.

1 Assemble twenty-one silver Tripoli formations (see page 63), each consisting of twenty 20-gauge rings, and fourteen silver Byzantine chain formations (see page 44), each consisting of fourteen 20-gauge rings. Following Steps 1 and 2 of the Trapezoid Key Fob (page 117), combine three Tripolis and two Byzantine chain lengths with one 16-gauge bronze ring (shown in copper).

2 Add two 16-gauge bronze rings (shown in copper), one each at the two left points of the first Trapezoid formation, as shown, and add a paperclip to the upper one to identify a beginning point.

3 Add two 16-gauge bronze rings (shown in copper), one each at the two right points of the first formation (Step 2), then add on two Tripolis and one Byzantine chain length to begin the second Trapezoid form. Notice that the form has its Byzantine chain sections on the bottom, opposite those on the first form, which are on the top, establishing the alternating pattern.

4 Add one 16-gauge bronze ring (shown in copper) to connect the two Tripolis added in Step 3, then add one Byzantine chain length (Step 3) to this ring and then a third Tripoli.

5 Add on the second Byzantine chain length by disassembling and reassembling its end pair rings (shown in copper) to the center 16-gauge ring, completing the second Trapezoid form.

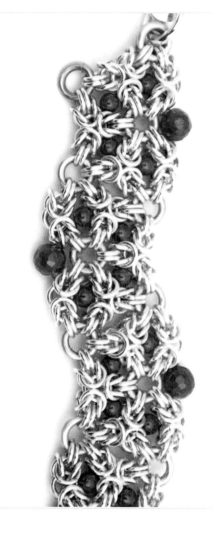

6 Continue adding Tripolis and Byzantine chain lengths with 16-gauge rings, following Steps 3–5, until you have seven alternating Trapezoid formations (a 7-inch bracelet chain length).

7 Bead each Trapezoid following Steps 4–9 of the Trapezoid Key Fob (see page 117), setting four 3.3mm beads within the Trapezoid formation and a single 5mm bead at the top of each form, between the two Byzantine chain sections. Add the S-clasp and catch rings (see page 29).

7 | Pentagon Formations

In this chapter, we assemble Tripoli formations and Byzantine chain sections into a variety of five-sided geometric patterns. We start with the basic Pentagon formation, and how to bead it in the Pentagon Key Fob. Once we've mastered the basic form, we'll make a Double Pentagon Bracelet with Pentagons made of two different metals and embellished with two different mineral beads, finished with a two-tone Double chain. The Pentagon Necklace exploits the repetitive Pentagon pattern with a centerpiece of five golden Pentagons, set with red garnet beads, and finished with a simple Single chain. The Pentagram Necklace features a beaded copper Pentagon surrounded by five beaded silver Tripoli forms that create a Pentagram formation that is finished with a bronze Jens Pind chain.

ASSEMBLING THE PENTAGON FORMATION

The Pentagon formation, the building block of most of the jewelry projects in this chapter, is assembled from five Tripoli formations that are connected with six pairs of rings: one pair in the center and one pair at each of the five points of the Pentagon. This basic Pentagon can be embellished with gemstone beads and combined with various chain designs, single or multiple.

1 Assemble five Tripoli formations (see page 63), each consisting of twenty 18-gauge silver rings. Combine four of the five Tripoli forms with a single 16-gauge gold ring (shown in copper).

Tools: Two flat-nose pliers, chain-nose pliers, and side cutters.

Materials: One hundred 18-gauge, 3.5m ID silver jump rings; twelve 16-gauge, 4.5mm ID gold-fill jump rings; five 4.5mm blue lapis lazuli beads; 5-inch length of beading cable; and a crimp tube, for one Pentagon formation.

2 **Left:** In the same place and parallel to the first 16-gauge ring (added in Step 1), add a second 16-gauge gold ring (shown in copper), connecting all four Tripoli forms. To close the second ring, place the tips of the chain-nose pliers on top of the right side of the open ring and below the already closed first ring and gently squeeze the ring closed.

3 **Right:** To close it flush and flat, use two pairs of chain-nose pliers, one in each hand, and grip the second ring on both sides with the pliers' tips and push/pull the ring closed.

4 **Left:** To add the fifth Tripoli form, disassemble the ending ring pair (shown in copper) of the fifth Tripoli and add it to the two 16-gauge rings connecting the other four Tripolis.

5 **Right:** Add ten 16-gauge gold rings (shown in copper), two rings connecting each of the five points of the Pentagon.

Beading the Pentagon

6   Start adding beads by running the beading cable through the upper-left Tripoli, and then add a single bead onto each side of the beading cable.

7   Run the cable through the next Tripoli and add the next bead. Continue adding beads in this manner until you have added all five beads.

8   After adding the fifth bead, run the cable through the fifth Tripoli and add a crimp tube to the end of the cable. Run the beginning of the beading cable through the crimp tube in an overlapping circle.

9   Pull both cable ends taut and smash the crimp tube with the chain-nose pliers. For extra security, run both ends of the beading cable through the next set of beads before trimming off the excess beading cable with side cutters.

The Pentagon formation can be easily converted to a key fob with a split key ring and a 14-gauge, 5.5mm ring to connect it.

DOUBLE PENTAGON BRACELET

The Double Pentagon Bracelet combines two Pentagon formations—the first made of bronze metal, embellished with five green chrysoprase beads, and the second of silver, with five red carnelian beads, giving the bracelet focal point two layers of duality. Once beaded, the double form is finished with a two-tone Double chain (a third layer of duality).

Tools: Two flat-nose pliers, two chain-nose pliers, and side cutters.

Materials: Two hundred 19-gauge, 3.1mm ID jump rings (one hundred bronze and one hundred silver); eighty 16-gauge, 4mm ID jump rings (forty bronze and forty silver); one 14-gauge, 5.5mm ID bronze catch ring; two 5-inch beading cables; two crimp tubes; ten 4mm beads (five green chrysoprase and five red carnelian); and one silver S-clasp, for an 8-inch bracelet.

1 **Left:** Assemble ten Tripoli formations (see page 63), five bronze and five silver, each consisting of twenty 19-gauge rings. Combine the five bronze Tripolis with one 16-gauge silver ring, following Steps 1–4 of the Pentagon formation (see page 122).

2 **Right:** Add three 16-gauge silver rings (shown in copper), connecting three of the five points (top, upper left, and bottom left) of the Pentagon, as shown.

3 Add two 16-gauge rings, one bronze and one silver (shown in copper), to connect the fourth and fifth points of the bronze Pentagon (upper and lower right), and add the first three silver Tripolis, beginning the second Pentagon form.

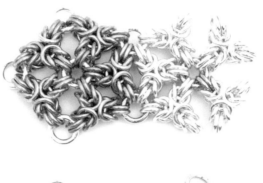

4 Add one 16-gauge bronze ring to connect the three silver Tripolis added in Step 3, and then add the fourth silver Tripoli to the same 16-gauge rings. To add the fifth Tripoli form, disassemble its ending ring pair (shown in copper) and add it to the same 16-gauge ring.

5 Add three 16-gauge bronze rings, one each connecting the remaining three points of the second (silver) Pentagon, as shown, completing the Double Pentagon formation.

6 Using one beading cable for each Pentagon, embellish the bronze Pentagon with the five green chrysoprase beads and the silver Pentagon with the five carnelian beads, following Steps 6–9 of the Pentagon formation (see page 123).

7 Assemble the remaining 16-gauge bronze and silver rings 2+2+2+2 into a Double chain (see page 156), alternating pairs of bronze and silver rings. Add the chain to the ending (point) ring of the silver Double Pentagon, as shown. Complete the bracelet with a silver S-clasp and catch ring (see page 29).

PENTAGON NECKLACE

The Pentagon Necklace continues the repetitive Pentagon pattern by assembling five golden Pentagon forms into a curved formation as the centerpiece to the necklace. Each of the five Pentagons is set with five red garnet beads and finished with two lengths of a simple Single chain that connects with a golden magnetic clasp to create a stylish necklace.

Tools: Two flat-nose pliers, two chain-nose pliers, and side cutters.

Materials: Five hundred 20-gauge, 2.75mm ID gold jump rings; twelve 16-gauge, 3.5mm ID bronze rings (used in the center of each Pentagon and on the outside edges); eight 16-gauge, 4mm ID gold rings (used to connect one Pentagon form to another); one hundred twenty-four 16-gauge, 2.75mm ID gold rings (for the Single chain necklace length); twenty-five 3.3mm red garnet beads; five 5-inch beading cables; five crimp tubes; and one gold magnetic clasp, for a 16-inch necklace.

1   Assemble twenty-five Tripolis (see page 63), each consisting of twenty 20-gauge gold rings. Assemble the first two Pentagon formations following Steps 1–5 of the Double Pentagon Bracelet (see page 125), but you will use two sizes of 16-gauge connector rings here: Connect the five Tripolis in the center of the Pentagon with one 16-gauge, 3.5mm gold ring, and join the three outside Tripoli points (top, upper left, and lower left) of the first Pentagon with 16-gauge, 3.5mm rings. Complete the remaining two outside points (upper left and lower left) of the first Pentagon, while adding on the first three Tripolis of the second Pentagon with two 16-gauge, 4mm rings. Combine the previously added three Tripolis with one 16-gauge, 3.5mm gold ring, and join the next two Tripolis to complete the second Pentagon form.

2   Add one 16-gauge, 3.5mm ring to the bottom point of the second Pentagon. Add two 16-gauge, 4mm gold rings (shown in copper) to connect the fourth and fifth points of the second Pentagon (added in Step 1), then add three gold Tripolis to begin the third Pentagon.

3   Add one 16-gauge, 3.5mm gold ring (shown in copper) to connect the three gold Tripolis added in Step 2, then add the fourth gold Tripoli. Add on the fifth gold Tripoli by disassembling and reassembling its end pair of 20-gauge rings (shown in copper) to the center 16-gauge ring to complete the third Pentagon.

4   Repeat Steps 2 and 3 two more times to add the fourth and fifth Pentagon formations to the repeating Pentagon curved-chain formation.

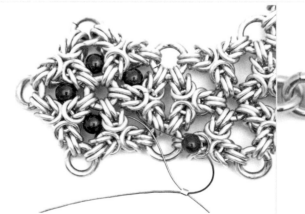

5   Using one 5-inch beading cable per Pentagon, embellish all five Pentagons, each with five red carnelian beads, following Steps 6–9 of the Pentagon formation (see page 123).

6   Assemble two 7-inch lengths of Single chain, 1+1+1+1 (see page 156), with the 16-gauge, 2.75mm gold rings. Add the magnetic clasp (see page 38) to combine two ends of the Single chain. Add the opposite ends of the Single chain to the ending points of the repetitive Pentagon formation to complete the necklace. **Note:** I made this magnetic clasp with five magnetic beads (versus the typical three) on both sides to make it superstrong for this high-end necklace.

PENTAGRAM NECKLACE

The Pentagram Necklace starts with a copper Pentagon formation that is set with five black onyx beads. This inner copper Pentagon is then surrounded by five silver Tripoli forms, each set individually with three black onyx beads, to create a beaded Pentagram formation. The Pentagram centerpiece is completed with two lengths of bronze Jens Pind chain and finished with a bronze S-clasp.

Tools: Two flat-nose pliers, two chain-nose pliers, and side cutters.

Materials: One hundred 20-gauge, 2.75mm ID copper rings; one hundred 19-gauge, 3.1mm ID silver rings; one hundred seventy-eight 16-gauge, 4mm ID bronze rings; one 16-gauge, 3.5mm ID copper ring (center of copper Pentagon); three 15-gauge, 5mm ID bronze catch rings; twenty 3mm black onyx beads; six crimp tubes; six 5-inch beading cables; and one bronze S-clasp, for a 16-inch necklace.

1   Assemble five 20-gauge copper Tripoli formations (see page 63), each consisting of twenty 20-gauge rings. Assemble five 19-gauge silver Tripoli formations, each consisting of twenty 19-gauge rings. Combine the five the copper Tripolis into a Pentagon following Steps 2–4 of the Pentagon formation (see page 127) using one 16-gauge copper ring.

2   Add five 16-gauge, 4mm bronze rings to connect the five points of the Pentagon formation. Using the beading cable, embellish the Pentagon with the black onyx beads following Steps 6–9 of the Pentagon formation (see page 123).

3   Using one beading cable and one crimp tube for each, embellish the five silver Tripolis with three black onyx beads, following Steps 1–9 of the Simple Beaded (3) Tripoli formation (see page 67).

4   Open one 16-gauge bronze ring on the upper right of the Pentagon and add on two beaded silver Tripolis via their ending ring pairs.

5   Open the upper left 16-gauge bronze ring and add the third beaded silver Tripoli. Continue adding the fourth and fifth beaded silver Tripolis to the 16-gauge rings of the Pentagon formation to complete the Beaded Pentagram.

6   Assemble two 7-inch lengths of Jens Pind chain (see page 71), using the 16-gauge, 4mm bronze rings, and connect them to the top 16-gauge bronze rings of the Pentagram. Add the bronze S-clasp and catch rings (see page 29) to complete the necklace.

8 Organic Formations

In this chapter we assemble geometric chain designs into organic shapes. We will start with a basic Beaded Fish formation that is made from a four-way Clover formation that extends on two points and is then set with an 8mm bead. This Beaded Fish formation is then assembled in a repeating pattern to create the Fish Bracelet, Necklace, and matching Earrings, which are set with a variety of faceted beads. The four-way Clover formation also lends itself to the Byzantine Cross formation, by extending just one of its four points; the golden Cross Earrings are set with blue quartz beads. The radial power doesn't stop at fours as we move to Five- and Six-Pointed Snowflake formations that are each set with a variety of yummy gemstone beads and combined in a somewhat random pattern into a wide Beaded Snowflake Bracelet. Next is the Butterfly formation, which combines every trick in the book to make an amazing beaded Butterfly centerpiece between two lengths of Byzantine chain in the Beaded Butterfly Necklace.

ASSEMBLING THE BEADED FISH FORMATION

The Beaded Fish Formation starts with a four-way radiating "Clover" formation that assembles four Byzantine knot formations from a center ring. Similar to the Tripoli formation with three radiating knot formations, the Clover needs a larger center ring to accommodate the fourth knot formation. This Clover is then extended on two of the four knot formations with Byzantine chain lengths to create a hollow, diamond-shaped interior filled with a gemstone bead.

Tools: Two flat-nose pliers, two chain-nose pliers, side cutters, and a paperclip.

Materials: Fifty-six 18-gauge, 3.5mm ID bronze jump rings; two 16-gauge, 4.5mm ID bronze jump rings; one 8mm blue turquoise bead; one 5-inch beading cable; and two crimp tubes.

Assembling the Clover Formation

1 **Left:** Add eight (four pairs) 18-gauge rings (shown in copper) onto a single 16-gauge bronze center ring, as shown.

2 **Right:** Add eight 18-gauge bronze rings, two onto each of the four pairs added in Step 1, creating four 2+2 chain sections (for knot formations) radiating from the center 16-gauge ring.

3 **Left:** Fold back and angle open each of the four 2+2 knot formations (Step 2)—one is shown here, held open with a paperclip. Add eight 18-gauge rings (shown in silver), two through each of the four knot formations.

4 **Right:** This is the completed Clover form, radiating four Byzantine knot formations from a center ring, which is the basis for the upcoming Fish and Cross chain patterns.

5 **Left:** Add eight 18-gauge rings (shown in copper), assembled 2+2, onto the two right four-knot formations of the Clover form, beginning the next Byzantine chain knot formations.

6 **Right:** Fold back and angle open each of the 2+2 knot formations added in Step 5—one is shown here, held open with a paperclip—and then add two 18-gauge rings (shown in silver) through each knot formation to extend the Byzantine chain.

7 **Left:** Add eight 18-gauge rings (shown in copper), assembled 2+2 (as you did in Step 5), beginning the next Byzantine knot formations.

8 **Right:** Fold back and angle open each of the 2+2 knot formations added in Step 7—one is shown here, held open with a paperclip—and add two rings (shown in silver) through each knot formation to extend the Byzantine chain.

9 Add eight 18-gauge rings (shown in copper) just as you did in Steps 5 and 7.

10 Fold back and angle open each of the 2+2 knot formations added in Step 9, and add a 16-gauge ring through both knot formations to complete the Fish formation.

11 Note that I unhooked the second 16-gauge ring, added in Step 10, to make Steps 11 and 12 easier. Run the 5-inch length of beading cable through the first 16-gauge ring in the center of the Clover formation (Step 1), but *not* through any of the 18-gauge rings. Bring both ends of the cable together in the center of the Fish formation, add a crimp tube over both ends of the cable, and adjust the cable so one end is only an inch in length.

12 While gripping both cable lengths in one pair of chain-nose pliers, use the second pair to push the crimp tube snug against the first (center) 16-gauge ring, and smash the crimp tube. Add the second 16-gauge ring back to the end of the Fish formation, as you did in Step 10.

13 Add the 8mm turquoise bead onto both lengths of beading cable, trim off the shorter (inch long) length of cable just past the turquoise bead, and add a second crimp tube to the one remaining cable.

14 **Left:** Run the cable through the second (ending) 16-gauge ring and then back through the second crimp tube and the turquoise bead.

15 **Right:** Pull the cable taut with one pair of chain-nose pliers and use a second pair to smash the second crimp tube tight against the bead.

16   While gripping the cable with one pair of chain-nose pliers, use the side cutters to trim off the excess beading cable. This is your finished Beaded Fish formation.

To create a key fob, add a split key ring to either the tail (through the ending 18-gauge ring pair of the Clover), or the mouth (through the outer [second] 16-gauge ring, below right). You can also connect the key fob to the fish formation with a chain length, below left.

Fish Collection Earrings

BEADED FISH COLLECTION

The beaded silver Fish Bracelet, Necklace, and Earrings featured on these pages were created as a private commission from a collector in New Jersey. Once you've mastered the basic Beaded Fish formation, these pieces can be assembled very easily.

The Fish Collection Bracelet assembles seven Beaded Fish formations, each connected mouth to tail through ending ring pairs, in a repetitive pattern. The bracelet is completed with an S-clasp (see page 29) connected via a 15-gauge ring to the last Fish's tail and two catch rings connected 1+1 from the first Fish's mouth. The bracelet (and necklace) are set with four different types of gemstone beads: black onyx, red quartz, purple amethyst, and blue quartz. All four are 6mm in size with faceted angles for more sparkle to complement the silver chain.

Fish Collection Bracelet

Fish Collection
Necklace and Earrings

Fish Collection Necklace centerpiece

Fish Collection Bracelet detail

Tools: Two flat-nose pliers, two chain-nose pliers, side cutters, and a paperclip.

Materials for silver bracelet: Three hundred ninety-two 19-gauge, 3.1mm ID silver jump rings; fourteen 17-gauge, 4mm ID silver jump rings; three 15-gauge, 5mm ID silver catch rings; seven 6mm faceted quartz beads (various colors); seven 5-inch beading cables; fourteen crimp tubes; and one silver S-clasp, for an 8-inch bracelet.

Materials for silver necklace chain: Seven hundred eighty-four 19-gauge, 3.1mm ID silver jump rings; thirty-one 17-gauge, 4mm ID silver jump rings; four 15-gauge, 5mm ID silver catch rings; fourteen 6mm faceted quartz beads (various colors); fourteen 5-inch beading cables; twenty-eight crimp tubes; and one silver S-clasp, for a 18-inch necklace.

Materials for silver necklace centerpiece: Fifty-six 18-gauge, 3.5mm ID silver jump rings; two 16-gauge, 4.5mm ID silver jump rings; one 8mm faceted amethyst bead; one 5-inch beading cable; and two crimp tubes.

Materials for silver earrings: One hundred twelve 19-gauge, 3.1mm ID silver jump rings; four 17-gauge, 4mm ID silver jump rings; two 6mm faceted blue quartz beads; two 5-inch-long beading cables; four crimp tubes; and two 2-inch-long, 19-gauge silver headpins for the earring backs.

The Fish Collection Necklace is assembled from fifteen Beaded Fish formations—two seven-fish bracelet lengths of 19-gauge fish, connected by one larger 18-gauge Beaded Fish centerpiece that is set with an 8mm faceted purple amethyst bead. To bring symmetry to the necklace design, the two bracelet lengths of the repeating Fish pattern mirror each other, and they bring focus to the larger Fish centerpiece. The two ending fish of the chain lengths are connected to the centerpiece via three 17-gauge, 4mm rings in a simple triangulation.

The collection just would not be complete without a matching pair of Fish Collection Earrings, set with 6mm faceted blue quartz beads and finished with 19-gauge silver earring backs (see page 34).

BYZANTINE CROSS EARRINGS

The Byzantine Cross Earrings are also based on the four-point Clover formation with four Byzantine knot formations extending from a single center ring. One of the four knot formations is extended with a Byzantine chain into a Cross formation, which is then embellished with four 5mm blue quartz beads.

Tools: Two flat-nose pliers, two chain-nose pliers, and side cutters.

Materials: Seventy-two 19-gauge, 3.1mm ID gold jump rings; two 17-gauge, 4mm ID gold jump rings; eight 5mm blue quartz beads; two 5-inch beading cables; two crimp tubes; and two 2-inch-long, 19-gauge gold headpins for the earring backs.

1 **Left:** Following Steps 1–4 of the Beaded Fish formation (see page 132), create a Clover formation, using 19-gauge rings (ending pairs shown in copper) connected with a single 17-gauge ring.

2 **Right:** Add twelve 19-gauge rings, extending one of the four Clover's points by two Byzantine knot formations to complete the Byzantine Cross formation.

Beading the Byzantine Cross

3 Run the 5-inch beading cable through four rings of the first knot formation of the Clover point that you assembled in Step 1 and extended in Step 2, and add two 5mm beads, one onto each side of the cable.

4 Run both lengths of beading cable up through the adjacent knot formations, first traveling through three rings (the angled-open and the ending pair) of the knots, as shown, then continuing the cable through the fourth (angled-open) rings of the knots so the cable is tight to the Clover formation, as when you beaded the Simple Beaded (3) Tripoli (see page 67).

5 Add two 5mm beads, one onto each side of the cable. Run one end of the cable through the next knot formation, traveling through three rings (one angled open and the ending pair) as shown. Run the opposite end of the cable through the single (angled-open) fourth ring, as shown.

6 Add the crimp tube to one end of the cable and then run the opposite end of the cable through the crimp tube in an overlapping circle.

7 Pull both cables taut and smash the crimp tube, which will be situated inside the ending ring pair at top of the Cross formation. Run both cable ends through the opposite beads and then trim off the excess cable with side cutters.

8 Add the small loop of the earring back to the ending ring pair at the top of the Cross formation. Repeat Steps 1–8 to make a second Byzantine Cross earring for a matching pair.

FIVE-POINTED SNOWFLAKE

The Five-Pointed Snowflake formation continues the technique of radiating Byzantine knot formations from a center ring. Related to the three-point Tripoli and the four-pointed Clover, the Five-Pointed Snowflake requires a larger diameter center ring to allow the fifth knot formation. The Snowflake will be set with five 4mm beads between each knot formation.

Tools: Two flat-nose pliers, two chain-nose pliers, and side cutters.

Materials: Forty 19-gauge, 3.1mm ID bronze jump rings; one 16-gauge, 4mm ID bronze center ring; five 4mm red carnelian beads; one 5-inch beading cable; and one crimp tube, for each Five-Pointed Snowflake.

Assembling the Five-Pointed Snowflake

1 Assemble four Byzantine chain sections (see page 44), each consisting of eight 19-gauge rings. Combine the four Byzantine chain sections with a single 16-gauge ring (shown in copper).

2 Add six 19-gauge rings (shown in copper), assembled 2+2+2 from the center 16-gauge ring, to create a fifth knot formation.

3 Fold back and angle open this fifth knot formation (see page 44), and add two 19-gauge rings (shown in copper) through the knot formation to complete the Five-Pointed Snowflake formation.

Beading the Five-Pointed Snowflake

4 **Left:** Run the beading cable through one of the five Byzantine chain sections, traveling through two rings within the knot formation, and add a 4mm bead.

5 **Right:** Continue running the beading cable through each Byzantine chain section, adding a 4mm bead between each section.

6 After adding the fifth bead, add the crimp tube onto one end of the beading cable. Run the opposite end of the cable through the crimp tube in an overlapping circle.

7 Pull both ends of the beading cable taut and smash the crimp tube with the chain-nose pliers. If possible (the drilled hole of the 4mm bead may be too small to allow this), run the cable ends through the neighboring beads, and then trim off the excess cable using side cutters.

The Five-Pointed Snowflake formation can be assembled in a repeating pattern to create bracelets and necklaces or combined with earring backs for a sparkling pair of earrings.

8 Repeat Steps 1–7 to create additional Five-Pointed Snowflake forms. Try different metal and bead combinations, such as bronze with red carnelian, copper with green chrysoprase, and silver with purple amethyst.

SIX-POINTED SNOWFLAKE EARRINGS

The Six-Pointed Snowflake formation extends the technique of radiating Byzantine knot formations from a center ring even further. Related to the Five-Pointed Snowflake, the Six-Pointed Snowflake allows a sixth knot formation to radiate from the center ring by stepping down to smaller 20-gauge Byzantine chain sections. The Snowflake will be set with six 3mm beads, one between each knot formation.

Tools: Two flat-nose pliers, two chain-nose pliers, and side cutters.

Materials: Ninety-six 20-gauge, 2.75mm ID gold jump rings; two 16-gauge, 4mm ID gold center ring; two 19-gauge, 1½-inch silver headpins for earring backs; twelve 3mm black onyx beads; two 5-inch beading cables; and two crimp tubes.

Assembling the Six-Pointed Snowflake

1 Assemble five Byzantine chain sections, each consisting of eight 20-gauge rings. Combine the five Byzantine chain sections with a single 16-gauge center ring (shown in copper). You will need to use the tips of two chain-nose pliers to close this center ring.

2 Add six 20-gauge rings (shown in copper), assembled 2+2+2 from the center ring, beginning the sixth knot formation.

Beading the Six-Pointed Snowflake

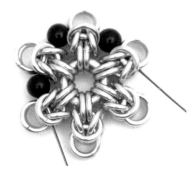

3 Fold back and angle open this sixth knot formation (see page 44) and add two 20-gauge rings (shown in copper) through the knot formation to complete the Six-Pointed Snowflake formation.

4 Run the beading cable through one of the six Byzantine chain sections, traveling through two rings within the knot formation, and add a 3mm bead to the cable. Continue running the beading cable through each Byzantine chain section, adding a 3mm bead between each section.

5 After adding the sixth bead, add the crimp tube onto one end of the beading cable.

6 Run the opposite end of the cable through the crimp tube in an overlapping circle. Pull both ends of the beading cable taut and smash the crimp tube with the chain-nose pliers. If possible (the drilled hole of the bead may be too small to accommodate), run the cable ends through the neighboring beads, and then trim off the excess cable using side cutters.

7 Repeat Steps 1–6 to create a matching earring, then add the earring backs (see page 34). Try different metal and bead combinations, such as silver with red carnelian, gold with black onyx, and copper with clear quartz.

BEADED SNOWFLAKE BRACELET

The Beaded Snowflake Bracelet combines the Five-Pointed and Six-Pointed Snowflake beaded formations in what would seem to be a chaotic pattern, but in fact it is quite organized, keeping a consistency in positive/negative spacing throughout the bracelet length.

Tools: Two flat-nose pliers, two chain-nose pliers, side cutters, and two paperclips.

Materials for each Five-Pointed Snowflake: Forty 19-gauge, 3.1mm ID jump rings (forty silver for each silver form, forty bronze for each bronze form, and forty copper for each copper form); one 16-gauge, 4mm ID center ring (one silver for each silver form, one bronze for each bronze form, and one copper for each copper form); five 4mm beads (five amethyst for each silver form, five red carnelian for each bronze form, and five green chrysoprase for each copper form); one 5-inch beading cable; and one crimp tube.

Materials for each Six-Pointed Snowflake: Forty-eight 20-gauge, 2.75mm ID jump rings (forty-eight gold for each gold form, forty-eight silver for each silver form, and forty-eight copper for each copper form); one 16-gauge, 4mm ID center ring (one gold for each gold form, one silver for each silver form, one copper for each copper form); six 3mm beads (six black onyx for each gold form, six red carnelian for each silver form, and six clear quartz for each copper form); one 5-inch beading cable; and one crimp tube.

Material for connecting all the Snowflakes: Forty-seven 16-gauge, 4mm ID jump rings (six copper, twenty-one bronze, and twenty silver).

Before you begin: Create a total of eleven Five-Pointed and eight Six-Pointed Snowflake formations (see pages 140–143). Make three Five-Pointed bronze with red carnelian beads, four Five-Pointed silver with amethyst beads, and four Five-Pointed copper with green chrysoprase beads. Make four Six-Pointed gold with black onyx beads, two Six-Pointed silver with red carnelian beads, and two Six-Pointed copper with clear quartz beads.

1 Assemble two Five-Pointed Snowflake formations (one bronze, one silver) and one gold Six-Pointed formation together with three 16-gauge rings. Each ring will connect the three Snowflake forms in a center triangle, as shown. Add a paperclip to create a beginning point to this three-Snowflake form to save your sanity.

2 Add two 16-gauge rings, one connecting the Five-Pointed bronze Snowflake to the Five-Pointed silver Snowflake at the top, and the second ring connecting the Five-Pointed bronze Snowflake to the Six-Pointed gold Snowflake at the bottom. This will force the three-Snowflake formation into a more-or-less triangle shape.

3 Assemble a second triangle shape of three Snowflake formations (one Six-Pointed gold, one Five-Pointed copper, one Five-Pointed bronze) exactly as you did in Steps 1 and 2 (don't forget the paperclip).

4 Assemble a third triangle of three Snowflake formations (one Five-Pointed silver, one Six-Pointed silver, and one Six-Pointed copper), as you did in Steps 1 and 2 (don't forget the paper clip).

5 After you've made three triangles (Steps 1–4), plan out a linear pattern by lining up the triangles, keeping an alternating pattern of metal and gemstone types.

6 Connect the first and second triangles with one 16-gauge bronze ring between the Five-Point silver and the Five-Point copper Snowflakes and one 16-gauge silver ring between the Six-Point gold and the Five-Point copper Snowflakes. Combine the second and third triangles with one 16-gauge bronze ring between the Six-Point gold and the Five-Point silver Snowflakes and one 16-gauge silver ring between the Five-Point bronze and the Five-Point silver Snowflakes.

7 Add an extra Snowflake between each of the three-Snowflake triangles assembled in Step 6. Add (first) Six-Point copper Snowflake on *top* between the first and second triangles with one 16-gauge bronze ring to the Five-Point silver of the first triangle, one 16-gauge silver ring to the Five-Point copper of the second triangle, and one 16-gauge bronze ring to the Six-Point gold of the second triangle. Add (second) Five-Point copper Snowflake on the *bottom* between the second and third triangles, with one 16-gauge silver ring to the Five-Point bronze of the second triangle, one 16-gauge bronze ring to the Five-Point silver of the third triangle, and one 16-gauge silver ring to the Six-Point copper of the third triangle.

8 Using the remaining Five-Pointed and Six-Pointed Snowflakes, assemble a fourth triangle with one Five-Point bronze, one Six-Point gold, and one Five-Point copper Snowflake. Assemble a fifth triangle with one Five-Point silver, one Five-Point copper, and one Six-Point gold Snowflakes. Assemble the fourth and fifth triangles onto the bracelet length (assembled in Steps 6 and 7). Add on the third extra Snowflake (Five-Point silver) between the third and fourth triangles and a fourth extra (Six-Point silver) between the fourth and fifth triangles, as you did in Step 7. Finally add the S-clasp and catch rings (see page 29).

BEADED BUTTERFLY NECKLACE

The Beaded Butterfly Necklace is, to me, the highlight of this book, a culmination of years of research and development in Byzantine chain derivatives and the different ways to connect chain to create unusual shapes. Starting with three Tripoli forms and two Byzantine chain sections that radiate from a center ring, each chain is then extended with varying Byzantine chain lengths that connect into an organic butterfly pattern with four large voids to be filled with gemstone beads. The beads are set in two layers: the first sets the outer beads and the largest inner beads, while the second adds pairs of smaller beads to fill in the gaps and give another level of depth to this winged beauty.

Assembling the Butterfly Formation

1 Assemble two Byzantine chain sections (see page 44 or 156), each consisting of fourteen 19-gauge rings. Assemble three Tripoli formations (see page 63), each consisting of twenty 19-gauge rings. Combine the two Byzantine sections and three Tripoli formations with a single 14-gauge ring (shown in bronze).

Tools: Two flat-nose pliers, two chain-nose pliers, and side cutters.

Materials for Butterfly formation: One hundred ninety-two 19-gauge, 3.1mm ID sterling silver jump rings; one 14-gauge, 7mm ID sterling silver center ring; four 16-gauge, 4mm sterling silver jump rings; two 10mm purple amethyst beads; two 6mm blue quartz beads; four 4mm red carnelian beads; one 4mm black onyx bead; four 3mm red carnelian beads; four 3mm black onyx beads; two beading cables (one 10-inches long and one 5-inches long); and three crimp tubes.

Materials for necklace chain (two 7½-inch Byzantine chain lengths): Four hundred thirty-six 19-gauge, 3.1mm ID silver jump rings; two 16-gauge, 4mm ID sterling silver catch rings; and a silver magnetic clasp, for a 16-inch necklace.

2 Assemble a total of forty-eight 19-gauge rings (shown in bronze), twelve onto each of the four upper lengths of the Tripolis from Step 1, to extend each by two more Byzantine chain knot formations.

3 Add four 16-gauge rings (shown in copper), two rings connecting each chain pair added in Step 2, to form the upper wings of the Butterfly formation. These pairs will also serve to connect the necklace length of chain.

4 Assemble a total of forty 19-gauge rings (shown in bronze), fourteen onto each of the outer Tripoli points (to extend each by three more Byzantine chain knot formations), and four rings assembled 2+2 onto each of the inner Byzantine chain sections. Notice that all four chains end in the 2+2+2 chain pattern, which will allow each of the four chains to be folded back and angled open so the chain pairs can be connected into a Tripoli formation in Step 5.

5 Fold back and angle open each chain's knot formation (see Connecting Byzantine Chains, page 49) and combine the chain pairs, as shown, with a pair of 19-gauge rings. Then add on four more 19-gauge rings (shown in copper), assembled 2+2 onto the previous pair. Fold back and angle open the copper knot formation, as shown, and complete the Tripoli with a pair of 19-gauge rings (shown in silver), completing the lower wings of the Butterfly formation.

6 Start with the 10-inch beading cable and add a 4mm black onyx bead to serve as the head of the butterfly. Run both ends of the beading cable from the outside to the inside of the upper wings, traveling diagonally through four rings within the Byzantine chain.

7 Add two 10mm purple amethyst beads, one onto each end of the beading cable, and then run each cable from the inside of the upper wings to the outside of the Butterfly form, traveling diagonally though four rings within the Byzantine chain, then add two 3mm red carnelian beads, one onto each cable end.

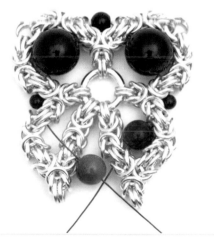

8 Run the beading cable from the outside to the inside of the lower wings, and add two 6mm blue quartz beads, one onto each cable end. Run both cables from the inside of the lower wings to the outside of the Butterfly form between the lower wings, again traveling diagonally through four rings within the Byzantine chain.

9 Add one 3mm red carnelian bead onto each of the cables; run each cable outward through the bottom of the Tripoli, traveling through three rings, (the *inside* angled ring and then the ending connector pair). Add a crimp tube, as seen at left. Keeping the crimp tube within the ending connector pair, run each cable through the single *outside* angled-open ring of the bottom Tripoli formation and then back through the crimp tube (within the connector pair), then through the *inner* angled-open ring and then through the previously added 3mm carnelian bead, as seen at right. This feat of cable gymnastics positions the crimp tube so it will be hidden within the ending connector pair of rings. Pull each cable taut and smash its crimp tube with the tips of the chain-nose pliers, and then trim off the excess cable with the side cutters.

Beading the Inner Butterfly Formation

10 Start with the 5-inch beading cable, run it through the upper Tripoli form, and add four 4mm red carnelian beads, two onto each end of the cable. Run each end of the cable down through the side Tripoli forms, from the upper wings to the lower wings.

11 Add four 3mm black onyx beads, two onto each cable. Run each cable through the lower Byzantine chain sections from the inside of the lower wing to the outside of the Butterfly form, between the lower wings.

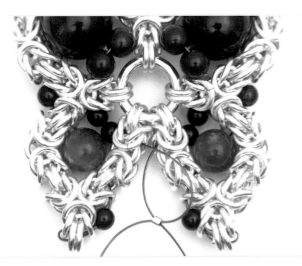

12 Add a crimp tube to one end of the beading cable and run the opposite cable end through the tube in an overlapping circle.

13 Pull both cable ends taut and smash the crimp tube with the chain-nose pliers. Run both ends of the cable up through the lower wings and trim off the excess cable with side cutters.

Assembling the Byzantine Chain and Finishing

14 For the necklace, assemble four hundred thirty-six 19-gauge rings into two 7½-inch lengths of Byzantine chain (see page 44 or 156). Connect both chain lengths to the Butterfly's upper pair of 16-gauge rings. Complete the necklace by connecting the opposite ends of Byzantine chain with catch rings and a magnetic clasp (see page 38).

The butterfly formations can be made in a variety of metals and gemstones and can be connected by a variety of chain lengths. This bracelet features a simple 1+2 chain with an S-clasp closure.

Appendix

In this section, we explore working with Argentium silver in more detail, and I give you a tutorial on how to make your own headpins using a simple hot-torch teardropping technique. I've created illustrated chain configurations as quick visual references to all the chain patterns used in the jewelry pieces in this book and present all of them in one layout, so it will be easy for you to identify, at a glance, the differences and similarities among the chains and the special characteristics of each.

WORKING WITH ARGENTIUM SILVER

Invented by Peter Johns in 1996, Argentium sterling silver is a silver alloy that offers numerous advantages over traditional sterling silver. Traditional sterling is 92.5 percent silver with the remaining 7.5 percent mostly copper. Argentium sterling is also 92.5 percent pure silver, but some of the copper has been substituted with a metalloid called germanium. This small amount of germanium, when heated, migrates to the silver's surface, where it combines with oxygen to form a thin layer of germanium oxide, which creates a barrier that prevents the copper from oxidizing and tarnishing the silver the way it does traditional silver. This germanium oxide barrier also lessens reticulation (wrinkling) of the silver's surface, so that heated Argentium wire can pull up into a perfectly smooth teardrop-shaped ball. Using this technique, known as teardropping, the studio jeweler can create aesthetically pleasing headpins from any gauge of Argentium wire.

Hardening Wire with Repeat Bending

Half-hard 19-gauge Argentium sterling silver wire is a bit too soft off the coil for me, so I harden and straighten it by bending it slightly with repeated pulls. Uncoil 3 feet of wire and, using flat-nose pliers, hold one end in your nondominant hand. Using a bandana over your dominant hand to reduce friction, pull the wire down its entire length. Start each pull at the pliers and pull evenly to the wire's end, adjusting your thumb's position to bend the wire against its original curve. On the final few pulls, equalize the thumb-to-first-finger pressure so the wire is pulled straight. After a dozen pulls, the wire should be straight and quite a bit springier than before.

You can pull three times the wire by placing one end of a 10-foot-long wire in a bench vise (substituting the vise for the pliers) and walking backward while using your finger pressure (through a folded bandana) as described above.

Cutting Wire Lengths

Using side cutters, cut multiple 4$^{1}/_{2}$-inch, 19-gauge wires. Mark and cut one 4$^{1}/_{2}$-inch length and then use it as your template for cutting the remaining 4$^{1}/_{2}$-inch lengths.

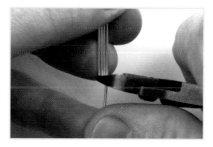

The 4$^{1}/_{2}$-inch wire becomes a 4-inch length when you terminate it with one teardropped ball at each end; cut into two 2-inch headpins. (A 3$^{1}/_{2}$-inch wire makes two 1$^{1}/_{2}$-inch headpins.)

PROPANE TORCH

A hardware-store propane torch works better than a proper oxyacetylene jeweler's torch for this technique because you need to bring the wire to a stationary flame instead of using the conventional technique of bringing the flame to the metal. If you use an oxyacetylene torch, attach the handpiece to a vertical support to keep the flame stationary.

TORCH PRECAUTIONS

Before using a hot torch for the first time, please seek advice and a demonstration from your local handyman or hardware store, and please take the following precautions:

1. As the wire heats up, it will burn your fingers, so hold the wire in a pair of pliers.
2. If you work a lot of wires, heat can conduct through the pliers and melt the plastic handle guards, so switch out pliers when they get warm.
3. Melting metal emits toxic fumes, so always work in a well-ventilated studio. I use a fan that blows across my face to dissipate the fumes.

HANDCRAFTING TEARDROPPED HEADPINS

Equip your workspace with a propane torch, a lighter, pliers, a pile of 19-gauge Argentium sterling silver wires, and a warm metal or stone, non-burnable surface on which to lay down the hot wire. I recommend you dim the lights to better see the subtle color changes of the Argentium as it transforms from a solid to a liquid state.

With your pliers in your dominant hand, hold the wire length in the middle, bring the tip of the wire to the tip of the blue flame, and count to three slowly: The wire will turn orange and you'll see a quick flash of liquid shine as it melts and is pulled upward and swells in size, forming a teardrop at the wire's end. Pull the wire out of the flame as soon as that intense orange flash appears. As the teardrop cools (another three seconds) keep the wire vertical, bead end down, to prevent the wire behind the teardrop from sagging to one side.

To teardrop the other end of the wire, turn your pliers over 180 degrees so the first teardrop is now pointing upward. Repeat the three-second heating and cooling process above. Place the heated, and still quite hot, double-teardropped wire down on a warm non-burnable surface, such as Solderite or ceramic, and let it cool slowly. Do not cool the wires in water or set them down on a cold surface, as the thermal shock will cause the teardrops to pop off the wire.

Finishing Teardropped Headpins

Before making earrings or setting gemstones with your new headpins, you must heat treat them in the oven (see page 18), clean them of oxidation by pickling, and polish them to a brilliant shine in a steel-shot tumbler. **Note:** It's important to finish your headpins before you assemble them into jewelry because some semiprecious stone beads would be damaged by these heating and polishing techniques.

RESOURCES

Wire Suppliers

Rio Grande in Albuquerque, NM
1-800-545-6566
www.riogrande.com
(noble and base metal wire—gold, silver, copper, brass, and bronze)

Hoover & Strong in Richmond, VA
1-800-759-9997
www.hooverandstrong.com
(noble metal wire—golds and silvers)

Hauser & Miller in St. Louis, MO
1-800-462-7447
(noble metal wire—golds and silvers)

E. B. Fitler in Milton, DE
1-800-346-2497
(base metal wire—copper, brass, and bronze)

Bead Suppliers

Rio Grande in Albuquerque, NM
1-800-545-6566
www.riogrande.com

Fire Mt. Gems in Grants Pass, OR
1-800-423-2319
www.firemountaingems.com

House of Gems
www.houseofgems.com

Earthstone
www.earthstone.com

Bonita Creations
www.bonitacreations.com

Magnetic Arts
www.magneticarts.net

Hand Tool Suppliers

Rio Grande in Albuquerque, NM
1-800-545-6566
www.riogrande.com
(exclusive retailers for Swanstrom pliers)

Otto Frei in Oakland, CA
1-800-722-3456
www.ottofrei.com

Jewelry Supply
www.jewelrysupply.com

Progress Tool
www.progresstool.com

Precut Jump Rings
APAC Tool in Providence, RI
1-401-724-6090
www.apactool.com
(kerf-less jump rings, headpins, S-clasps, and my supply kits)

Spider Chain in San Francisco, CA
1-510-368-0646
www.spiderchain.com
(saw-cut jump rings in multiple metals and sizes)

Headpins, S-Clasps, and Magnetic Clasps

APAC Tool in Providence, RI
1-401-724-6090
www.apactool.com
(19-gauge headpins, jump rings, S-clasps, and my supply kits)

Rotary Tumbler
Lortone Tumblers in Mukilteo, WA
1-425-493-1600
www.lortone.com

Three-Prong Chuck
www.davidchain.com/toolkit.html

Publications

Art Jewelry
www.artjewelrymag.com

Lapidary Journal Jewelry Artist
www.lapidaryjournal.com

***American Craft* Magazine**
www.craftcouncil.org

Author Contact and Links to Other Artists' Sites

Scott David Plumlee
Email: info@davidchain.com
www.davidchain.com

CHAIN CONFIGURATIONS

Chain configuration tutorials are available in click-through graphics on my website: www.davidchain.com.

Single chain

Double chain

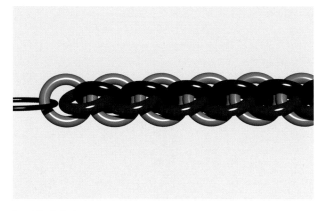

Jens Pind chain

Byzantine chain—open knot form

Byzantine chain—folded knot form

1+2+1 chain

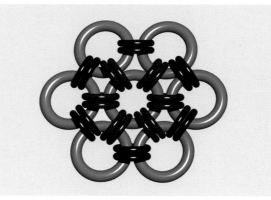

Japanese 12-1 chain

Inca Puño—open knot form

Inca Puño—folded knot form

Small Flower formation—three rings

Large Flower formation—four rings

INDEX

SCOTT DAVID PLUMLEE has been inspiring a new generation of chain jewelers over the past decade, publishing books and leading workshops nationwide. His previous books, *Handcrafting Chain and Bead Jewelry* and *Chain and Bead Jewelry Creative Connections*, are best sellers in the jewelry-making field. A world traveler and jack-of-all-trades, Scott has studied ancient cultures and craft designs all over the globe and currently resides in sunny Taos, New Mexico.

"I challenge myself to create innovative chain designs by utilizing curiosity as a guide and creativity as a catalyst to find new solutions to the age-old puzzle of how to combine metals and gemstones. Over the past decade, I have found that the path of least resistance in creating new designs is simply to be aware of the possibilities within the happy accident and explore my imagination with reckless abandonment. By employing creativity, I can turn the intangible images in my mind from sketchbook into beaded metal wire creations that are comfortable to wear and stunning to behold."

Scott David Plumlee